KT-133-777

The life laundry:

How to de-junk your life

The life laundry:

How to de-junk your life

Dawna Walter
and Mark Franks

This book is published to accompany the television series
The Life Laundry, produced by Talkback Productions and first
broadcast on BBC2 in 2002.
Series editor: Daisy Goodwin
Series producer: Susie Worster

Published by BBC Worldwide Ltd
Woodlands
80 Wood Lane
London W12 0TT

First published 2002
Reprinted 2002 (seven times), 2003 (twice)
Copyright © Talkback Productions Limited 2002
The moral right of Dawna Walter and Mark Franks to be identified as the
authors of this work has been asserted.

All rights reserved. No part of this book may be reproduced in any
form or by any means, without permission in writing from the publisher,
except by a reviewer who may quote brief passages in a review.

ISBN 0 563 53475 3

Commissioning Editor: Nicky Copeland
Project Editor: Sarah Lavelle
Art Director: Lisa Pettibone
Design: Grade Design Consultants
Picture Researcher: Victoria Hall

Set in Helvetica Neue and OCRB
Printed and bound by Imprimerie Pollina, s.a. L 90947
Colour separations by Kestrel Digital Colour, Chelmsford

BBC Worldwide would like to thank the following for providing
photographs and permission to reproduce copyright material. While
every effort has been made to trace and acknowledge all copyright
holders, we would like to apologize should there have been any errors
or omissions.
Abode 10, 86; BBC 6, 110 (Mike Hogan); *BBC Good Homes* magazine
34, 44, 58, 66, 72, 76, 80, 88, 90, 93, 96, 98, 100, 102; *BBC Homes
& Antiques* magazine 46; Andreas von Einsiedel 2; The Holding
Company 52, 62; Lu Jeffrey 131, 134.

Contents

Introduction

It is an extraordinary experience to be invited into people's homes to help them sort through their junk. It is also very brave of them to allow strangers like myself to go through their most personal items and, as often as not, unearth the traumas behind the clutter.

Obsessive clutter is often a symptom of underlying emotional issues. Unless you are able to get to the root of the problem, the symptoms are likely to return. Letting go of your junk is the best way of taking the first step towards recovery and confronting the real issues that cause you to hold on to things.

Although we may not all be excessive hoarders, we all have an issue with clutter in some area of our lives. It may be confined to a small area of your home, such as a particular cupboard that attracts junk, or not knowing how to cope with a pile of paperwork. Gaining control of these areas can free up space and time for more important matters in your life.

I have spent the last seven years advising families throughout the world on how to store things in their homes and get systems in place to organize their lives. During this time I have visited many homes and spoken with many people who had lost control of the things going on around them. Material possessions and other debris had taken over their physical space, and the clutter was disrupting their ability to carry on a normal life.

Some issues could be solved by simply assigning a place to everything in the home, then encouraging the discipline to put things away daily. There are many clever products on the market that can increase the storage capacity within each clutter hotspot. Other solutions involved space planning and a complete overhaul of how furnishings work in the context of the room. However, I still found that some problems could not be solved in this manner.

My interests led me to study Reiki, a Japanese system of healing. Through this practice, I have become more aware of how emotional and mental issues in our lives can affect how we function physically. These types of issues can cause our physical space to be cluttered with many reminders of the past, or can deprive us of the motivation to take charge of the clutter in our lives. In many cases it can even cause physical symptoms of stress or other illnesses. By taking action to address these problems, it is possible to let go of the emotional and physical clutter and move on to a greater awareness of the present moment.

My co-author, Mark Franks, is no stranger to clutter. In his work as a clearance specialist and antique dealer, he has been into many homes and brought his particular skills at sifting, saving and discarding to bear on the accumulations of a lifetime.

The Life Laundry is a programme about the process of letting go of the unnecessary clutter in our lives. Each contributor to the series made a commitment to confront their junk on television and let go of everything but those items they used or really appreciated. We received many letters and videos from families around the country whose clutter had adversely impacted on their health, safety, and emotional well-being. Although we were able to visit only a handful of families, the clutter hotspots we found are common to most homes. Chapter 3 includes some case studies that might inspire you to confront your own problem areas. Wardrobes, understair cupboards, lofts and all the hiding places are uncovered and de-junked on pages 85–101.

The methods that Mark and I have used over the years to help clear space were incorporated into the real-life situations of our contributors. With the help of an amazing crew, we were able to remove years' worth of clutter from each home and help the occupants to confront their junk. By literally placing each family's life on the lawn, they could come to terms with all the junk they had accumulated over the years. There were often tears of remembrance, sadness and joy as they let go of the past and decided to make a fresh start.

By the time you notice that the clutter in your life is out of control, it is often such an enormous problem that it is difficult to know how and where to begin to get rid of it. This book will help to restore order in your life.

First you are guided through the causes of clutter and encouraged to find the ones that apply to you. Then you are helped to formulate a plan of attack and implement it. Along the way you can come to grips with your emotional attachment to clutter, then you can cast it off and even make some money in the process.

Take heart – you are not alone. We'll guide you every step of the way.

Dawna Walter and Mark Franks

Do you need to de-junk?

Holding on to things that no longer have a purpose is a problem common to most of us at some time in our lives. The hoarding may last only a short time and may perhaps have arisen from a situation in your life that happened during or before the time that things started to pile up. Then, as if a light has been turned on, you become aware of the situation and get things back on track.

Letting things pile up happens for a variety of reasons. Many of us would like to lead a less chaotic life but simply don't know where to begin. The most important thing to remember is that the problems of clutter are universal. All my years of experience dealing with organizational issues in homes worldwide has taught me that the clutter in our lives often comes from the same root causes.

Learned behaviour

We often mimic the behaviour that we learned as children growing up. Think back to your parents' home and see if you now find that you are simply repeating the patterns from your childhood. If this is the case and you are unhappy with the situation, re-educate yourself into developing a new routine. Become aware of how more positive role models manage to live in clutter-free environments and seek advice from those friends or family members whose houses are more of an example of how you wish to live. By becoming aware that you are just doing as you were taught, you will be able to teach yourself to organize your home more efficiently.

Space planning

A problem that I see every day in homes that simply have too much stuff is poor space management. I want to stress that this is probably the most common problem and requires nothing more than looking at where you place the furniture and objects in your home.

Good space management is a logical process, meaning that you place furnishings near the point where they are most used. Each item of furniture must serve a purpose in your home, and should be used only for that purpose.

The clutter hotspots found in every home are very predictable. The example that comes to mind is the very first thing you see on getting home – the hallway.

In almost every case I deal with, there is some sort of table or surface in the hallway that becomes a repository for everything imaginable: stacks of post, unwanted circulars, free newspapers, hats, clothes, umbrellas, food and rubbish. You name it and I have probably seen it stacked up near the front door.

This clutter is the first thing that confronts you when you get home. It also gives the first impression to anyone who visits your family. What does it say about you?

The simple solution is to decide what the table should be used for. Appropriate uses would be to keep one day's worth of post on it and provide a storage place for keys. It is fine to use the table in a decorative way with appropriate ornaments or photographs, as long as it remains dusted and tidy.

If you find that things continue to pile up even after addressing the problem, guess what? You must move the table.

Chapter 3 outlines all such clutter hotspots throughout your house and will help you with positive suggestions of how and where to place your furniture to minimize the dumping of unwanted stuff.

After completing the Life Laundry Survey at the end of this chapter, you will know what areas of your life need the most attention. Start with the easiest areas first and as you feel more positive, begin to tackle the more difficult areas. Lightening up the physical junk will help to lighten up the emotional junk.

Clutter blindness

In extreme cases, it is possible to lose sight of the problem until things get so out of control that the situation begins to affect your ability to get on with life. This can be manifested in various ways. For example, you might run out of space for your possessions or maybe you can never find what you're looking for.

Many people seem to be living in a fog and can't see the wood for the trees. This includes all the material things that no longer serve a purpose in your life, but are still taking up space and energy. They are often masking a more serious problem of holding on to past situations and emotions that you need to release in order to move forward.

Assessing the problem

In any situation, it is a good idea to assess the degree to which a problem impacts on your life. It might be having all kinds of effects – physical, mental, emotional and spiritual.

Becoming aware that your possessions are beginning to control your life can be the first step towards letting go of them. It means that you are choosing to live in the present, developing an awareness of all that is going on around you. By taking an objective look at this, it is possible to change your behaviour and improve on all aspects of your life.

Take a look at the following categories and see what best describes your situation.

Empty nesters

You have spent the last 20 years or so raising a family and now your children have reached the age when they are no longer living at home. For many of you, raising your children has been your primary job – you may have given up a career to focus all your energy on looking after the family.

Your routine has changed dramatically since the children left home. All the jobs that required so much time over the years have disappeared and you find that you are not quite sure what to do with your new-found freedom. You may lack energy and feel that your life no longer has the focus and meaning it had when the house was full of people.

Perhaps you'll want to preserve the memories of when your children were growing up. You might even leave their rooms exactly as they left them, almost as a shrine to a time when you perhaps felt that your life had more meaning.

You may even find yourself spending more and more time in their rooms, reliving the past. You have probably collected many souvenirs of your children's early years, such as clippings from their first haircut, their baby teeth, report cards, trophies, schoolwork, books, clothes, toys and games. The presence of these things enables you still to feel connected to your children and you find it difficult letting go.

Another common problem for empty nesters is that your kids leave home to start their own lives but have no room to store all their accumulated possessions, so they leave tons of their things in your home, piled up in the loft, stacked in your garage or shed and cluttering up your cupboards. What was once their room in your house becomes a repository for stuff they never make the time to go through and dispose of. Often it includes big objects, such as bicycles and stereo systems, which sit around collecting dust and prevent you from using the space as your needs now require.

Families with small children

When you are just starting out, you may be living in a house that you feel has suddenly become too small for your new family. The arrival of children requires clever storage solutions to enable you to put away all the new equipment in your life, such as prams, playpens, nappies and toys, along with all the other usual domestic items.

You may be part of a household in which both partners work, leaving less time to cope with the pressures of being a new parent. As children require so much effort, you may feel drained by the time they are put to bed and have little energy left to cope with the things that are accumulating around you.

The children's needs force you to focus on them rather than domestic matters. When you take a good look around, things seem to be piling up all over your house, but you can't seem to find the hours in the day to get it sorted.

Once the children have reached an age when they are walking, the situation can get even worse, with toys, books and games now spread throughout the home. You may have difficulty locating things, especially at busy times such as first thing in the morning, and this can start a cycle of stress before you even leave the house.

Young professionals

You and your partner both work in demanding jobs and seem to spend a lot of time away from home. You have no children, so your work seems to be the most important thing in your life. You worry about competition and making the grade, and spend your time off working from your home in an effort to keep up.

When you're not working you want to socialize, or perhaps you're too tired and simply slump in front of the TV.

Your mind is often in work mode and you don't seem to see what is going on around you in your home. You seem to collect tons of papers, which start to spread throughout the house and prevent you from using the rooms in your home for their intended purpose. You may subscribe to journals, magazines and papers but never seem to find the time to read them.

Basic household chores may suffer from a lack of attention. Finding clean clothes to wear might become a problem, or there never seems to be any food in the house. You may not be aware of the general situation in your household.

Students

Going away to university is your first experience of being independent. You live away from your parents and are now the master of your own fate. You are experiencing many new things going on around you and are faced with many temptations in lifestyle that wouldn't have been allowed at home. You may stay out late more often than you used to and find getting up in the morning more difficult. You might feel like you are always in a rush to get somewhere. Although you had to help with household chores when you were at home, you are now solely responsible for your cleaning, laundry or cooking.

You have limited room to store your things and may be sharing a space with other people. Your schedule might not be the same each day, making it difficult to develop a routine.

Divorcees and the newly single

Your life has been turned upside-down by your recent split. You have had to downsize your living arrangements significantly because of the economics of being on your own and you have quite a lot of things that you have accumulated during the course of your marriage.

In cases where the split is acrimonious, material possessions can become the battlefield for hurt egos. Things that you perhaps never used or enjoyed while you were together are suddenly the things that are very important to you now.

You have more things than space and find that you store many unopened boxes in a loft, garage or shed. You may find that you even have unopened boxes in the personal areas of your home, such as your bedroom and bathroom.

You surround yourself with memories of your past life and find it difficult even to think about entering a new relationship. You associate all your things with the life you once had and deeply resent having to move to another home.

If you are the one who remained in the shared home, you could have many of the same problems of association as the one who is forced out. Shared possessions will be a constant reminder of the life you once had, and you might hang on to them to create the idea that nothing has changed.

The recently bereaved

Bereavement can often cause us to hold on to the past and perhaps lose sight of what is going on in the present. It is an individual process that can take years to work your way through.

It is important to understand that there are common feelings and needs that most people experience upon the death of a loved one, or indeed, with any major loss. After the initial feelings of shock and numbness, you may experience intense emotions of fear, anger and sadness that could last for many months.

During this time you might find that you need help both emotional and practical. On the emotional level, you might find a greater need than usual to express your feelings both verbally and in writing. It helps to have close friends and family members who are good listeners around you. You may also need help doing practical things, such as making funeral arrangements or disposing of your loved one's personal effects. For many people it may be necessary to clear out possessions almost immediately after the loss, at a time when they are not ready for the process of sorting and letting go. Everything can end up in boxes and remain there for years.

This can be a very traumatic time that may stir up quite intense emotions of guilt, agitation, panic, irritability and restlessness. These can lead to sleeplessness, depression, withdrawal, despair and disorganization. Professional advice may be necessary to enable you to move forward. The process of going through personal items is an important part of coming to terms with bereavement. It allows you to think about the memories associated with each item, and with the support of family, friends or a professional counsellor, release some of the emotions that may be a deeper part of your grief. Far better to confront emotions when they occur rather than years down the road when they may have become a disruptive force in your life and adversely affected your mental, emotional, spiritual and physical health.

Single women

You live on your own and spend most of your weekdays out of the house working and socializing. Your priorities are more social than domestic, and the only thing that motivates you to focus on the way you are living is when you can't find what you need. This makes you feel harassed and out of control.

You don't really like being on your own, so you fill your time with lots of activities, such as shopping and meeting up with friends, to keep you out of the house and in the company of others. Being at home means you must confront the fact that you are on your own, and perhaps this makes you uncomfortable.

You find that you avoid dealing with things around your home until you run out of essentials, such as food and clean, ironed clothes, and are forced to tackle the situation. You may also find that you lose paperwork, fall behind in your bills and have a wardrobe packed with things you never wear – a testament to over-zealous shopping and poor money management.

Single men

You grew up in a family where your mother did most of the chores around the house, but now you are living on your own and have no one to look after you. You may not have purchased very much furniture and instead let things stack up in all areas of your home.

You take great care of the things that interest you, and spend a lot of your disposable income on home leisure and entertainment, such as CDs, computers and electronic equipment. However, you have not taken the time to develop a system of how to store them.

You accumulate newspapers to unmanageable proportions, let your unwashed laundry become critically inconvenient and have a tendency to throw your clothes on the floor rather than hang them up.

Your kitchen is a problem area, although you probably eat out or order take-away rather than cook. You sometimes allow dishes to sit in the sink for days before washing them, and the rubbish can get out of control.

Enough really is enough

What does it take to make you realize that enough is enough? I have seen many families whose lives have become completely out of balance because they are no longer able to cope with all their stuff. This results in a dysfunctional situation in the home, which can lead to both physical and emotional distress, sometimes ending in divorce.

The easiest way to explain how clutter can affect all levels of your being is through the theories of vibrational medicine which are based on Einstein's Theory of Relativity. As you may recall from your schooldays, Einstein's theory stated that all matter is made up of energy. My training in Reiki energy systems, a Japanese form of vibrational healing, has taught me that it is not only physical matter that consists of vibrations. All the other levels of our being – mental, emotional and spiritual – are also made up of vibrations.

If you have ever been to a homoeopathic doctor, you will know that remedies are prescribed on the basis of like curing like. Immunization also uses the same principle. Although homeopathy and orthodox medicine do not use the term 'vibration' in their teachings, the end result of like being used to cure like could be described as two like vibrations cancelling each other out.

If you can accept the viewpoint that matter vibrates, think about how much energy the extraneous matter in your household takes up. You have probably heard the expression 'bad vibes' or 'bad energy', which is used to describe an unpleasant atmosphere. All the vibrations of your possessions are taking up space and energy, leaving little room for new thoughts and fresh energy to enter your life.

Clutter in your life makes it much less likely that you will achieve all you set out to do. Being unable to start the process of shedding the junk, all areas of your life begin to suffer, and you may be left feeling like a ship without a rudder.

If each day becomes a chore and you seem to have no sense of direction, take a look at some of the more common ways listed below that clutter can impact on your day-to-day living.

Physical effects of clutter

The physical impact of clutter can be looked at in two ways – how your things are physically taking up space in your home and how your things physically affect your health.

- You try to find something and suddenly notice that there are too many things in the way. Getting hold of what you need becomes a time-consuming process.
- You have so much junk that you simply have no idea where things are located. You spend a lot of time hunting, but often without success.
- When you think about it, there are often quite a few incidents that may happen to draw your attention to what is going on around you (such as always tripping over the same pile of stuff and not moving it until you fall and injure yourself). Too often we just don't see these clear indications that all is not well.
- Clutter is oppressive and can affect your health in a negative way. If you are depressed or irritated by your environment, it may weaken your immune system and make you more susceptible to colds and flu. It might even result in more serious physical conditions.

Mental and emotional effects of clutter

Letting things pile up can have a dramatic effect on your mind.

- You might find that your mind wanders and you lack concentration, making it difficult for you to finish things. This can certainly be a major problem in your job.
- You may also feel that you don't have enough energy to begin a project. You feel tired most of the time and are generally lacking in motivation. You feel worn out before you begin.
- Your personal life can become strained and you may find it difficult to communicate with those around you. You may find that your emotional responses are exaggerated and out of proportion to the situation. You lose your temper or burst into tears with little provocation.

Old emotions associated with the inability to let things go are vibrations taking a toll on your mental and emotional health. Letting things go and releasing these vibrations leaves room for fresh energy and more constructive thoughts, enabling you to get on with your life. This is dealt with more fully in Chapter 4.

Common reasons for letting things pile up

Things often start to pile up in your life after some sort of change has occurred. It could have been a traumatic event, such as a bereavement, or something that you might have thought unimportant at the time, such as a forgotten birthday. Or it might have been a lifestyle change, an adjustment to the routine, such as moving to a new home, rather than a major problem.

It is important to try to remember when the situation began. Take a look at what was going on in your life at that time. Think about what happened several years before that. Most people can remember if they focus hard enough. Don't be surprised if something surfaces that seemed insignificant when it originally occurred. The mind sometimes has odd ways of processing information or dealing with unhappy events.

If the situation has not been resolved on the mental or emotional levels, it can manifest itself on the physical level in order to make us deal with it. Go with whatever comes into your mind, acknowledge all the emotions attached to it and allow yourself to let it go. Remember that releasing these old energy patterns will make room for a flow of new energy in your life. (See also Chapter 4 and the case studies on pages 80–1 and 109.)

The life laundry survey

This survey is designed to give you the opportunity to focus on the problem areas of your life and, most importantly, to empower you to take action to resolve them. It is worth taking the time to think about your answers. If you make the positive commitment to change your energy patterns, you will find that it is much easier to take the first step towards a happy and fulfilled life.

Before starting the survey, take a few minutes to relax your body and your mind. Simple breathing techniques can help to de-stress the body and calm the mind, often helping to release emotional blockages in the process. As we go through life, the stress that we accumulate from many types of situation affects our breathing and puts tension in our body.

Follow the breathing and stress-reduction techniques in Chapter 4 and choose the method that works for you. With a calm mind and relaxed body, focus on your intention to master your clutter. Start by thinking about each of the questions and how they relate to your current situation.

Getting to know your clutter

When clutter takes control of your life, it is often easier to block it out than deal with it. The purpose of getting to know your clutter is to make you aware of exactly how you view each cluttered area. Without visiting the area, mark your answers to each question in pencil. When you have completed the survey, go and visit each area, noting the difference between your mental picture and the reality.

1. **How much clutter is there in the area outside your house, e.g., driveway, front garden, side passage?**
    a. a great deal
    b. quite a lot
    c. some
    d. very little

2. **When you walk through the front door, does your hallway seem under control?**
    a. never
    b. rarely
    c. often
    d. always

3. **Do you put your keys in the same place each evening?**
    a. never
    b. rarely
    c. often
    d. always

4. **When you bring home newspapers or other reading materials, do you finish them the same day?**
    a. never
    b. rarely
    c. sometimes
    d. almost always

5. **Do you dispose of newspapers and magazines when you have finished reading them?**
    a. never
    b. rarely
    c. sometimes
    d. almost always

6. **Do you open your post each day and deal with it immediately, for example, checking bank statements or paying bills?**
    a. never
    b. rarely
    c. sometimes
    d. almost always

7. Looking at the surfaces in your hallway – tables, steps, floors or chairs – are they free of clutter?

    a. never
    b. rarely
    c. sometimes
    d. almost always

8. Standing in the doorway of your living room and looking inside, are you able to move around with ease?

    a. never
    b. rarely
    c. sometimes
    d. almost always

9. Do you have so much clutter that you can't easily access certain areas?

    a. everywhere
    b. quite a lot
    c. little
    d. none

If so, list the areas that have blockages, starting with the least bad area first.

1. _____
2. _____
3. _____
4. _____
5. _____
6. _____
7. _____
8. _____
9. _____
10. _____

10. Are you able to use the furniture for its intended purpose?

    a. never
    b. rarely
    c. sometimes
    d. almost always

11. If you have a video or DVD player, are the tapes and discs put back in their jackets and neatly stacked?

  a. never
  b. rarely
  c. sometimes
  d. almost always

12. What percentage of them have you watched in the past year?

  a. 10%–30%
  b. 30%–50%
  c. 50%–80%
  d. 80%–100%

List below any videos or DVDs that you have not watched in the past year. If you have more than 10, select those that you are unlikely to watch again.

1. _____
2. _____
3. _____
4. _____
5. _____
6. _____
7. _____
8. _____
9. _____
10. _____

13. Are all your music CDs, records and tapes kept in their sleeves and stacked so that you are able to find things easily?

  a. never
  b. rarely
  c. sometimes
  d. almost always

14. Are there articles of clothing in your living room?

  a. almost always
  b. sometimes
  c. rarely
  d. never

15. Does your living room reflect who you are?
   a. not at all
   b. a bit
   c. a lot
   d. completely

16. What percentage of the furniture and fittings in your living room do you actually use?
   a. 10%–30%
   b. 30%–50%
   c. 50%–80%
   d. 80%–100%

List below any items in your living room that you have not used in the last year.

1. _____   11. _____
2. _____   12. _____
3. _____   13. _____
4. _____   14. _____
5. _____   15. _____
6. _____   16. _____
7. _____   17. _____
8. _____   18. _____
9. _____   19. _____
10. _____   20. _____

17. Does your kitchen area seem to be under control?
   a. never
   b. rarely
   c. sometimes
   d. most of the time

18. Are you able to move around with ease?
   a. never
   b. rarely
   c. sometimes
   d. most of the time

19. Is there clutter preventing you from accessing any areas of your kitchen?

    a. everywhere

    b. quite a lot

    c. little

    d. none

If so, list the areas that have blockages, starting with the most accessible first.

1. _____
2. _____
3. _____
4. _____
5. _____
6. _____
7. _____
8. _____
9. _____
10. _____

20. How often are the worktops and surfaces free of clutter?

    a. never

    b. rarely

    c. sometimes

    d. almost always

21. How often are dirty dishes left in the sink?

    a. often

    b. sometimes

    c. rarely

    d. never

22. Does the rubbish bin get filled to overflowing before someone empties it?

    a. always

    b. usually

    c. rarely

    d. never

23. Do you have out-of-date food in your cupboards?
   a. often
   b. sometimes
   c. rarely
   d. never

24. Do you have out-of-date food in your refrigerator?
   a. often
   b. sometimes
   c. rarely
   d. never

25. Do you use the kitchen appliances you've acquired for their intended purpose?
   a. never
   b. rarely
   c. sometimes
   d. often

List below any appliances such as blenders and food processors, that you haven't used in the last year.

1. _____	11. _____
2. _____	12. _____
3. _____	13. _____
4. _____	14. _____
5. _____	15. _____
6. _____	16. _____
7. _____	17. _____
8. _____	18. _____
9. _____	19. _____
10. _____	20. _____

26. Are you able to find things in your kitchen when you need them?
   a. never
   b. rarely
   c. sometimes
   d. almost always

27. Looking into your bedroom from the doorway, does the room feel like it is under control?

    a. never
    b. rarely
    c. sometimes
    d. almost always

28. Is there clutter that prevents you from gaining access to all areas?

    a. many
    b. quite a lot
    c. few
    d. none

29. Is your bed made every day?

    a. never
    b. rarely
    c. sometimes
    d. almost always

30. Are the surfaces, including bed, chairs, bedside tables, lamps and floors, free from clutter?

    a. never
    b. rarely
    c. sometimes
    d. almost always

31. Does your bedroom reflect who you are?

    a. not at all
    b. a bit
    c. a lot
    d. completely

32. Do you hang your clothes up when you take them off?

    a. never
    b. rarely
    c. sometimes
    d. almost always

33. Are all the clothes in your wardrobe hung on hangers?
a. never
b. rarely
c. sometimes
d. almost always

34. Are the clothes in your drawers neatly folded?
a. never
b. rarely
c. sometimes
d. almost always

35. What percentage of your clothing have you worn in the last year?
a. 10%–30%
b. 30%–50%
c. 50%–80%
d. 80%–100%

List below all the items of clothing that you have not worn in the last year. If there are more than 20, list those you are not likely to wear again.

1. _____
2. _____
3. _____
4. _____
5. _____
6. _____
7. _____
8. _____
9. _____
10. _____
11. _____
12. _____
13. _____
14. _____
15. _____
16. _____
17. _____
18. _____
19. _____
20. _____

36. Do you keep your shoes in good condition?
a. never
b. rarely
c. sometimes
d. often

37. What percentage of your shoes have you worn in the last year?
  a. 10%–30%
  b. 30%–50%
  c. 50%–80%
  d. 80%–100%

List below all the shoes you have not worn in the last year.

1. _____
2. _____
3. _____
4. _____
5. _____
6. _____
7. _____
8. _____
9. _____
10. _____

11. _____
12. _____
13. _____
14. _____
15. _____
16. _____
17. _____
18. _____
19. _____
20. _____

38. Is the bathroom floor free of clutter?
  a. never
  b. rarely
  c. sometimes
  d. almost always

39. Are the sink and bath free of clutter?
  a. never
  b. rarely
  c. sometimes
  d. almost always

40. Do you check the bathroom cabinet for outdated cosmetics and medicines?
  a. never
  b. rarely
  c. sometimes
  d. often

41. If you have an airing cupboard, do you use it to dry your clothing?
  a. never
  b. rarely
  c. sometimes
  d. almost always

42. Do your children put their toys away?
  a. never
  b. rarely
  c. sometimes
  d. almost always

43. Does your laundry get out of hand?
  a. often
  b. sometimes
  c. rarely
  d. never

44. Do you have difficulty in parting with sentimental items?
  a. always
  b. sometimes
  c. rarely
  d. hardly ever

45. Do you spend time looking through keepsakes, such as old photographs or letters?
  a. always
  b. sometimes
  c. rarely
  d. hardly ever

46. Do you have difficulty in finishing projects?
  a. often
  b. sometimes
  c. rarely
  d. never

47. Do you deal with things when they happen?
   a. hardly ever
   b. rarely
   c. sometimes
   d. almost always

48. How often do you pursue your hobbies?
   a. never
   b. rarely
   c. sometimes
   d. often

49. Do you view shopping as a leisure activity?
   a. often
   b. sometimes
   c. rarely
   d. never

50. How often do you throw away things you don't use?
   a. never
   b. rarely
   c. sometimes
   d. often

51. Do you ever confront your junk and take action to clear the space?
   a. never
   b. rarely
   c. sometimes
   d. often

Energy and Physical Health Assessment

52. How energetic do you feel on waking up in the morning?
   a. need another hour in bed
   b. sluggish
   c. ready to face the day
   d. highly energetic

53. Do you have difficulty sleeping?
  a. often
  b. sometimes
  c. rarely
  d. never

54. If you have difficulty sleeping, do you find that you worry or try to solve problems at night?
  a. often
  b. sometimes
  c. rarely
  d. never

55. How do you feel you are coping with life?
  a. out of control
  b. definitely needs improvement
  c. generally pretty well
  d. happy and fulfilled

56. How is your general health?
  a. poor
  b. below par
  c. good
  d. excellent

Now count up your points as follows:
A = 10 points, B = 7 points, C = 4 points D = 2 points

100–150 points

You are well balanced and your household routines seem to be doing the trick. You may have more difficulties with time management than letting go of emotional junk. Go through your answers and look for any obvious patterns. Use the problem-solving methods on pages 38–40 to come up with ways of addressing the areas you wish to improve.

151–250 points

Your difficulties are more circumstantial and probably derive from bad habits. By focusing your attention on the problem situations and becoming conscious of your actions, you will be better able to develop a routine to get rid of the clutter. Review your answers to become more aware of the areas of your life that could use more structure. Apply the goal-setting method on pages 36–7 to make improvements to your bad habits.

251–400 points

Your life is in a downward spiral and you are unable to concentrate on getting things done. You have difficulty in finding things and have bad time-management skills.

  You have a hard time letting go of the past and have periods of depression. You may find that your physical health has started to deteriorate. It is time to take action to get your life back on track. Review your answers and make a list of the five areas that you would most like to change. Starting with the easiest first, go to the goal-setting section on pages 36–7 and look for the easiest, quickest and best solutions to get to the root of each problem, and take action to move forward in your life.

400+ points

You have taken the time to fill in the survey, so you are aware of the clutter problems in your life. You are ready to try anything as you have been unable to take the first step to get rid of the emotional and material junk. You probably have many friends and relatives who are aware of the problem and urge you to take action. Your physical and mental health may have suffered from a trauma that occurred before things started to get out of control. You sometimes feel in a dense fog, not connected to the present moment. You are ready for a big change. You are a perfect candidate for a clutter-busting weekend with the help of your friends and family, and any other emotional support you may need. Things can only get better when you confront your junk.

Getting started

Take action: taking action is the most immediate way to feel better about any situation. By focusing your attention on the situation, you bring yourself into the present moment and are able to look at what is going on around you.

All the contributors to the television series had to take the first step by writing to us for help with their clutter problems. This act alone showed intention. In addition to their introductory letter and photographs, they were required to meet researchers and members of the team to ascertain whether they were truly ready to commit to the process of letting go of their junk.

By filling in the Life Laundry Survey at the end of Chapter 1, you have taken the first step in gaining a greater understanding of the clutter problems in your life. In reviewing your answers, try to determine what habits you may have developed that contribute to the household clutter. Just learning to throw things away when you are finished with them can make a dramatic difference to your life. Taking action every day keeps the piles of stuff at bay. These are simple solutions that take just self-discipline and determination.

Time management

Everyone can do with better time management, as it is one of the most common causes of chaos in the home. The problem is not that you don't want to let it go, but simply that you can't find the hours in the day to stay on top of all the household demands. The easiest way to overcome this is to do a weekly plan and stick to it.

Go to your local office supply shop and take a look through all the diaries and time-management forms available. Select the format that you feel most comfortable with. I would recommend a weekly planner that has each day broken down into hours and allows you to see the entire week at a glance.

Begin by filling in your fixed commitments. These include getting to and from work, collecting kids, going to the gym and all the other routines that you are required to do on a daily and weekly basis. Allow an adequate amount of time to get to and from each commitment, not just the time that you are required to be present.

Now make a list of all the chores that seem to have got out of hand in your household and set a specific time to accomplish each one. Enlist the help of everyone in your household to clear the space and get rid of the stuff that has accumulated, then plan when and by whom each chore will be done.

Remember that committing your thoughts to paper is the first step towards resolving the problem. Developing a routine that you stick to without exception will help to teach you positive new routines that will become a habit.

Plan to do a little bit each day. Develop routines with members of your household to make sure that everything is attended to in the present when it happens. Make sure that everyone in the house knows where everything belongs and gets into the habit of putting things away after each use. Doing a bit every day ensures that the situation never gets out of hand. By focusing on your intention to finish each job that you begin, you will be on the right path towards living in a clutter-free environment.

Goal-setting

Not knowing where to begin can be the beginning of the problem. With our contributors, their goal was to complete the clutter-busting in the allotted time of the filming. We then set an intermediate goal for them to try to complete by the time we came back to revisit the situation.

Goal-setting is the best way to begin any project. It empowers you to identify problems and find solutions in a logical and pragmatic manner. Unfortunately, many people whom I encounter during the course of my work don't think enough about their problems.

Recognizing problems will enable you to find solutions, even when you don't think you are able to see any way forward. The process of recognition will help you on every level of your being – physical, mental, emotional and spiritual. As Simone de Beauvoir said, 'It is in the recognition of the genuine condition of our lives that we gain the strength to act and our motivation for change.'

Always try to solve the easiest problems first. As you begin to see and feel the impact of changes you have put into place, you can begin to tackle the more difficult emotional issues.

Chapter Four details some effective techniques for letting go of emotional clutter. Refer to the exercises when you feel that you need to understand the emotional issues that may be causing you to hold on to your clutter, or whenever you need to look at different ways of solving problems.

Clutter-busting goals

Physical clutter is generally easier to solve than emotional clutter. If you are determined, organized and throw enough help at the job, you can clear rooms' worth of debris over just a few days.

Review your self-assessment form and look at the worst clutter zones in your home. Make a list, beginning with the easiest areas first and ending with the most cluttered area of your home.

Next to each area that you need to tackle, write down your immediate goals (next seven days), short-term goals (next three months) and long-term goals (on-going programme). If the kitchen is one of your clutter hotspots, your goals could be:

Immediate: Clear the refrigerator and cupboards of all expired foods. Throw away all rubbish. Clean thoroughly.

Short-term: Throw away all broken china. Keep only the china that you use. Organize your cupboards.

Long-term: All surfaces are free from unwanted clutter. You only keep those things that serve a function or bring you pleasure. You find the space relaxing to be in.

Continue down the list of physical clutter zones in your home until you have written your clutter-busting programme for each area.

Problem solving

Once you have set your goals, you need to decide on the best solutions to achieve each goal.

Immediate and short-term goals are usually more action-orientated and require time and resources to put right. For example, if your immediate goal is to clear your refrigerator and cupboards, you must decide when you will do it and if you require any help. Intention and determination will enable you to complete the task.

Look for some solutions to your specific clutter problems in Chapter 3. Each problem area has exercises to help you shed your unwanted junk and should take several hours to complete. Always plan to give the project your undivided attention: it is important to see it through to completion. Take before-and-after pictures and then reward yourself by doing something that you enjoy.

Timetable

There are several ways to go about getting rid of your clutter. In the television series, we selected the areas of our contributors' homes that would make a dramatic improvement to their lifestyle, but could be achieved over a four-day period that included filming. The goal was to inspire them to continue the process in other areas of their homes.

Our contributors had to agree to sort through all their possessions and let go of everything but the essentials or things with sentimental value. There were tasks and goals that needed to be achieved each day.

The job for the first day was to identify the items for removal from their clutter hotspots, then to pack and transfer them to the lawn or driveway. This took extensive labour to achieve in the four hours allotted for its completion.

On day two, the contributors had to confront all their clutter in one location. This is a very emotional experience, which can be very embarrassing as well as eye opening.

The contributors have to go through each item in every box from each room in order to decide what goes back in the house.

The fast-paced method of confronting a lot of clutter at one time means that you must be certain you are ready to let things go: it is essential to be decisive or the exercise is wasted.

Our contributors were able to confront and release years' worth of junk that no longer served a purpose in their lives. Each of them was astonished to find items that had been unnoticed or buried for years, or taking up space in the wrong location. Mark found some hidden treasures and the flow of energy into all of the rooms was dramatically improved.

What to keep and what to bin

In all honesty, when clutter gets out of control in people's lives, most of the stuff they're holding on to is junk of little value. As Mark explains in Chapter 5, holding on to junk can be expensive because professional house clearances, of which he does many, cost money and generally turn up little of value.

Many people confuse sentimental value with cash value, particularly where inherited items are concerned. If you really believe your junk has value, follow Mark's suggestions in Chapter 5 to help you decide whether it should stay or go. If in doubt, consult a professional.

Another difficulty that assails people in assessing their junk is that they are forced to confront how much money they spend on things they never use. People often want to recoup some of their money by selling these unused items, but never get round to visiting a car boot sale or local antique dealer. They hold on to the junk in the belief that it will get better with age. In most cases, exactly the opposite happens.

When you see all your junk gathered in one place, you will find how many things you duplicate. This is often because you have no idea what you own. You keep purchasing the same things over and over because you are unable to find what you need when you need it. The answer? Bin all duplicates, keeping the one in the best condition.

When our contributors were faced with their lives on the lawn, they had to confront all their indulgences in one go. In most cases, about 20 per cent of the stuff had to go to the tip because it was in such bad condition that it had no value to anyone. Charities do not want damaged or broken items. See what they do want on page 131.

As in all the exercises, bin the easiest items first. Getting rid of bulky things and stuff that is really redundant will have a huge impact on your space.

Dispose of...

- Anything in the house that has been broken for 12 months or more.
- Anything that has exceeded its use-by date. Use suitable disposal methods for anything that is combustible or poisonous.
- All wonky furniture that is surplus to your needs.
- Any boxes that have not been opened since your last move.

Lots of junk, such as paper, glass, plastics and cans that have collected throughout your house, can be recycled and should be among the first to go. In many houses this stuff can account for another 20 per cent of the accumulated clutter. Find out your local authority's recycling schemes, and you can dispose of things quickly and safely.

Keeping on top of the situation

It is great to have an army of friends supporting you as you try to make a new beginning. You must, however, make the commitment to change your routines and take control so as not to fall back into bad habits. This is an integral part of the 12-step programme used in curing addictions, and one of the essential principles of Reiki. Both philosophies are based on the premise that you are able to control the situation one day at a time.

Planning a clutter-busting weekend

If you feel that you are now ready to let things go on a big scale, then a clutter-busting weekend can dramatically improve your living conditions. The key to success in this massive effort is good planning.

I recommend starting with the most accessible clutter hotspots in your home. If you plan to use a skip or disposal vehicle and have only limited use of it, get rid of the largest items first: this will have the greatest impact in clearing your clutter. Look at your answers to the Life Laundry Survey to help to decide the right areas to begin.

What to organize in advance

- Do you need a skip to remove large items?
- If so, does it require a permit or special lighting?
- Do you require a van or removals company?
- Will the council come at a specified time for large item removal?
- Do you know the hours of your local dump?
- Find out what items your local council recycles, and where and how they are collected.
- Check with your local charities to see what items they are able to accept. (Some will collect furniture and other bulky items.)
- Make a list of local antique dealers who will value any hidden treasures.
- Find out where and when your local car boot sale is held. Don't forget to ask whether it is cancelled in inclement weather.

What you need on the day

- Strong boxes with lids (you always need far more than you think).
- Newspaper for wrapping breakables.
- Rubbish bags.
- Sticky labels.
- Tags to identify contents and disposal method.

To make your clutter-busting weekend a memorable experience, gather together all the people you can count on to help – friends and family – the more the merrier. You might want to spend the night away from your home, just as our contributors did, because this can help you to view your possessions more objectively.

View the experience as moving out of your old life and into the new. If the clutter or problem areas are really horrendous, call in a removals crew to help you let it go.

Easy does it

If the thought of clearing a large area over a weekend overwhelms you, then develop your own tailor-made programme using the same planning principles and tools as required for the clutter-busting weekend.

Review your list of goals and clutter hotspots and choose an area that you feel ready to deal with. This can be something such as photographs or CDs, or a scary space, such as an airing cupboard. Set aside several hours of uninterrupted time to focus your attention on reducing your clutter by 50 per cent. Don't stop until you have reached that target. If you feel ready to clear the entire area, it will energize you to start the next project.

For the two weeks after you have reduced the clutter in an area, become aware of how the space now feels. Pay attention to whether you begin to collect clutter in the same places. If you do, repeat the procedure and try to reduce the clutter by 50 per cent. If clutter again accumulates after two weeks, repeat the procedure weekly. If it takes longer for the area to get cluttered, halve the amount of time the build-up takes, then again try to reduce the amount by 50 per cent. Continue on the programme until you are able to keep the area clutter-free.

The purpose of this exercise is to make you aware of the situation as a matter of routine. Cluttered areas are often blanked out and become invisible. To break that pattern, you need to remind yourself of the situation on a daily basis. A good way to do this is with positive affirmation. This takes the form of a giant note that you put somewhere you can see every day – perhaps a communal location like the kitchen or somewhere more personal, such as your wardrobe. The affirmation must be positive, in the present tense and concise. For example, 'My wardrobe is tidy' will immediately draw your attention to the condition of your wardrobe.

Long-term goals

Goals that are on-going require more thought and concentration in order not to slip back into old patterns.

The most important thing is to get your brain thinking about all possible solutions, without judging whether they are good or bad solutions. Not being able to solve a problem immediately can make some people stop thinking at all about ways to solve it. This is the most common reason that junk becomes invisible.

If your long-term goal is to have a kitchen that you can relax in, you might find the following suggestions will help you achieve that:

- Keep the kitchen clean.
- Use your kitchen only for cooking or entertaining.
- Spend more time planning dinner rather than eating fast food.
- Entertain more.
- Get a chair for the kitchen.
- Redecorate.
- Install some pot plants.

How to achieve your goals

If you are more logical than creative, do the following exercise to help you find ways to achieve your goals.

1. For each goal you have, write down three solutions to help you achieve it.
2. Write down another four solutions to achieving your goal without judging whether they are good or bad. Continue listing solutions until you can't think of any more.
3. Look at all the solutions you have listed and choose the easiest, quickest and best one to achieve your goal.

If you are a more creative type of thinker, you might find that visualizing helps you to find solutions.

1. Sit comfortably in a chair, feet on the ground, and back well supported.
2. Breathe in deeply, slowly and smoothly to the count of four, then release to the count of four.
3. Imagine a big flower with beautiful petals. In the centre of the flower is the issue you are trying to resolve. See the solutions

coming out of the centre of the flower and allow each to rest on a beautiful petal. Keep going until no further solutions come out of the flower, then write them down.

4. Pick the easiest, quickest and best solution for each of your goals.

Once you are able to see that there are many ways to achieve your goals, you can focus your attention on the situation and achieve all that you desire.

Review your progress

It is important to review your progress as you begin to let go of your clutter. Go back to each situation and periodically review how far you have progressed. Not all change is cataclysmic. The objective is to reduce the scores on your self-assessment and continue with the on-going programmes until you feel that you have your clutter under control.

Each time you tackle an area, remember to revisit it. Bring your awareness to the trouble spots every day to make sure you stay on top of the situation.

As you begin to shed your clutter, you must work very hard to change the habits that you may have fallen into over many years. It is not always possible to change these habits overnight.

It is unhealthy to hold on to the old, stale energy, emotions and physical reminders of things that happened in the past. They prevent you from living in the present, promote low self-esteem and can cause health problems on the physical level.

If you find it difficult to let go of certain areas of your clutter because of emotional attachments, the exercises in Chapter 4 will help you to quieten the mind and focus your attention. In this way you can get to the root of the problem and learn the necessary lessons to let go of the physical and emotional clutter.

3

Clutter hotspots

'Use it or lose it' is the motto for each clutter hotspot in your home. Go to the easiest and quickest area first to see how shedding some of your stuff makes an instant difference to how you feel and how your home looks. As you begin to feel the benefits, move on to the next-easiest areas for de-cluttering until your home is completely clutter-free.

Dedicate several hours for each project. It is important to focus on the job in hand and finish the entire area before moving on. If you find some areas difficult to tackle on your own, ask for help from someone whose opinion you value. Sometimes we need an extra push to keep us on track and help us to let things go.

Remember to have all the necessary equipment at hand to complete the task: boxes for items to be given away, bags for stuff to be thrown out or recycled. To really see the most impact from each project, plan to dispose of all your junk immediately. Evaluate the end result and note the improvements in your lifestyle.

3

Books

From the time we were children, books have played a significant role in our lives. Most of our earliest memories include being read to by our parents. Many of us are even able to remember our favourite stories, which we pass on to our own children.

Your current reading habits were probably formed by your early childhood. If reading played an important part in your youth, it will probably remain one throughout life. Books are often among our most treasured possessions. However, they do get out of control in many homes, spreading into many areas and quickly cluttering up the space. To gain control of the situation it is necessary to look at your current reading habits.

Books fulfil various functions in your life and home. Many people find reading one of the greatest forms of relaxation, as it triggers the imagination and allows the mind to escape the day-to-day pressures. Others may read to find information and insight. Whatever your reasons for reading, letting go of books that no longer represent the way you live or feel will empower you to take back the space for new ideas.

Paperbacks

Being cheap and available from all sorts of places, paperbacks are common impulse buys. Depending on where you buy from, there can also be a social element to purchasing a book. Some shops have coffee bars, and sell other items, such as CDs, stationery and cards, which may tempt you to linger.

Paperbacks are also attractive because new titles are heavily marketed, and reading the books that everyone is talking about makes you feel connected to the moment. It is also something that can be discussed and shared with friends and family. It does, however, promote buying more than you may have time to read.

I have very strict rules about paperbacks. Once read, only the most meaningful are kept: everything else gets recycled. Charity shops will gladly accept used books in reasonable condition, or you can pass them on to your friends. When I go on holiday, I always leave my paperbacks in the hotel for other guests to use.

Hardbacks

Since hardbacks are expensive purchases, it is often difficult to convince people to part with them. Many believe that because they seem more substantial, they will go back and read them again. The truth is that most of them sit on the shelf gathering dust.

There are many ways to recycle hardcover books that you no longer use. Second-hand bookshops will buy copies in good condition, and this can generate some money to replace them with books that interest you at this time of your life.

Hardbacks also make great gifts to friends, especially if you know that they would find the book useful or interesting. Write your name inside and pass it on to someone you think would appreciate it. Suggest they add their name inside and continue the process. Knowing that others will benefit is a great motivator to letting things go. Local libraries and schools are always appreciative of book donations. Think about how many people can then enjoy your generosity.

Sometimes we use books to fulfil purposes other than reading. Coffee-table books full of beautiful pictures can inspire our creativity or put us in a peaceful frame of mind.

Beautiful books can be used as a design feature in your home to help create atmosphere. Stack them on a table in the sitting room or in a special corner of your bedroom. Use them as a mental calming tool and recreate some of the beautiful images that you find inspirational.

Keep illustrated books out of direct sunlight and dust them often to prevent the paper from deteriorating.

Reference books

Far too often we hang on to reference books as collector's items rather than reference tools. Many of them represent rites of passage from earlier times in our lives: think of that encyclopedia set you had in school, your old textbooks or job-related reference books. Long after we have stopped needing them, they remain as trophies in the bookcase.

Travel guides, cookbooks, and self-help manuals all contain valuable information meant to be retained. If, however, you haven't used them in the past few years, lose them to make room for the new interests in your life.

USE IT OR LOSE IT: BOOKS

If you find that books are invading your space, get rid of the rubbish and save the treasures.

GOALS
TO RECYCLE ALL BOOKS THAT YOU NO LONGER USE AND RECLAIM SPACE THROUGHOUT YOUR HOME. TO UNDERSTAND YOUR READING HABITS AND DEVELOP POSITIVE PURCHASING STRATEGIES.

BENEFITS
- Getting rid of your outdated ideas and ways of thinking opens you up to new and exciting possibilities that enable you to learn new things, regardless of your stage of life.
- By looking at the things that interest you in your current lifestyle, you stay connected to the moment rather than living in the past.
- By rationalizing your books and retaining only those you value, you will free up space throughout your home.

TOOLS
- Sturdy cardboard boxes. Don't get them too big or overfill them or you'll never be able to lift them.

METHOD
Set aside an afternoon to complete this project in one go.
Enlist all members of the family who contribute to the problem.

1. Determine the best way to dispose of each item.

2. Strike the quickest and easiest target first. In the case of book clutter, trashy novels come high on the list, so go on a search-and-discard mission in every room of your house. Gather up all your paperbacks in one location and have the intention of reducing the quantity by 90 per cent.

3. Keep any books that you genuinely use for reference, any that have sentimental value, and any that you feel still have lessons to teach. You may also keep a limited selection for your guest room, and you should encourage your guests to take them when they leave.

4. Go through the remaining books and put aside any that you wish to pass on to friends. Make sure you hand them over immediately.

5. Put the remaining books in sturdy boxes. If you regularly attend car boot sales, place the boxes in an out-of-the-way location with any other items that you have prepared for the sale. There are lots of great tips about sales on pages 126–30. All other boxes should be immediately taken to your local charity shop or other good cause.

6. Gather all the remaining books in your house to where most are stored. Don't forget to root them out of all the scary places, such as under the stairs or in the loft. Have the intention of reducing the remaining books by 50 per cent.

7. Start by removing all the contemporary hardbacks that you have finished and are unlikely to read again. Box them up to go to the second-hand bookshop, friends and family.

8. By this time, you will have disposed of most of your books and be left only with those dear to you. Before you replace them on the shelves, be sure to dust both the shelves and the books. Things that you keep on display must always be well maintained.

9. Organize the books so that reference titles and those most frequently used are in the most accessible locations; those used less frequently can be kept on the higher shelves that are more difficult to reach.

10. To help you find particular titles easily, develop a system of organization that makes sense to you. If you think about how a bookshop or library is arranged, you might want to adapt their system of dividing books into categories, then alphabetizing them by author.

11. Now that you are able to see your life in books, think about who you have been and who you are now. Take the great leap and let go of some of the trophy books that we all keep to remind us that we have obtained knowledge. You don't need the status symbol of a book to know what you have achieved in your intellectual pursuits.

12. If you have complete collections of classic books that you are ready to let go of, they may be more valuable than current literature. Go to a reputable book dealer to ascertain the value of the books. There are some helpful hints in Chapter 5.

13. Children must learn to appreciate the value of their books and look after them. As they get older and outgrow their old stories, suggest they pass them on to those less fortunate. Donate the books to your local hospital, charity shop or playgroup.

GOOD PLACES FOR READING

Once you have decided what books to keep, it is important to keep them in the most suitable location in the house. To do this you need to take a look at your reading habits. Think about keeping cookbooks in your kitchen, reference books in your office and current literature by the side of your bed or in your living room. By consolidating them into fewer locations, you regain valuable space and keep them from getting out of control.

Many people read at bedtime. It can release your mind from day-to-day concerns by providing intellectual stimulation or escapism. But for those who have difficulty sleeping, reading in bed is a pattern that needs to be broken. It can act as a stimulant that prevents the mind from resting, so you must re-educate yourself that bed is for sleeping, not reading. If you suffer from insomnia, it is advised that you get out of bed and go to another room to read.

If you find that the most relaxing reading location in your home is the bedroom, limit your selection to current reading materials or those inspirational and motivational books that you seek for guidance.

A favourite chair in the sitting room is a great place to curl up and relax with a book. Limit each family member to keeping only one book at a time in any place other than their own room to prevent books from taking over the house again.

ON–GOING PROGRAMME

For the next two weeks pay attention to how and why you purchase your books. To help you answer, consider the following questions:
• Do you purchase books when you are waiting for public transport?
• How many of your book purchases are planned rather than impulsive?
• Do book reviews and magazines influence your purchases?
• Do you enjoy the social aspects of your local bookseller?
• Do you read all the books you purchase?
• Do you read more than one book at a time?
• Do you ever re-read books that you have collected?
   If so, how many of your books have you re-read in the last year?

If you find that you compulsively purchase more books than you are able to read, try to set a monthly book budget and stick to it. If you find that you enjoy the social aspects of visiting the bookshop, plan to spend time browsing rather than shopping.

Decide that for every book you purchase, you will give one away. Sticking to these rules means that books will never again take control of your space.

Entertainment

Like books, CDs and videos play an important part in stimulating your imagination and relaxing your mind. Music creates atmosphere and is an important ingredient at every good party. For many it is an alternative to television. We can therefore justify purchasing music because it keeps us entertained.

As technology has developed, so have the ways of listening to music. I often encounter redundant collections of vinyl when going through people's clutter, and cassette tapes are fast heading the same way. Some people, however, are collectors of vinyl, CDs and tapes, which means that they must make efficient use of space to store and care for them properly.

The problem of entertainment becomes even more complicated when you look at how many areas of the home have entertainment units. It is not uncommon to find some method of playing music in each room of the house. And don't forget the portable players you might take when you go out.

When you add it all up, you could well find that music is one of your largest monthly purchases. How much of it do you actually listen to? To get control of your music collection, it is necessary to focus on your purchasing and listening habits.

Music, like books, constantly evolves, with many new releases each day. We are bombarded with music in every area of life, from walking down the street to getting in a lift or waiting for someone to pick up the phone. It is no surprise that when we hear a tune that sticks in our head, we go out and buy it.

The process of buying music has never been easier. Many bookshops also have a section for CDs, and music stores are designed to keep you inside for a very long time. Interactive systems allow you to listen before you purchase, which is a good idea to make certain that you will listen to the music when you get it home.

More and more people are using the Internet to shop for music or to download it directly to their computer. The easier and less costly it is to obtain, the more you are likely to collect.

Organizing your music

How you arrange your music collection will often dictate what you listen to most often. When no system is in place and your collection is scattered about, you often can't remember what you own. You defeat the relaxing qualities of the music by having to spend ages trying to find what you want.

There are several ways to organize your music: the first is alphabetically by artist, the second is alphabetically by category. It's a good idea to group like with like – classical music in one area, rock in another – then alphabetize by artist within the category. You may find that you listen to classical music in the bedroom and rock in the sitting room. By paying attention to your listening habits, you can save time and space throughout the house. Use the same technique to organize the music you carry around with you or in your car.

Use or lose all the music that you no longer play (unless you are a collector). If you listen mostly to CDs, dispose of the cassettes or albums you haven't played in the last year. It may be difficult to part with these items because of the initial investment, so if this is keeping you from letting go, take them to a second-hand shop and pocket the cash.

Remember to protect your investment. If looked after properly, your music collection will last many years. Determine to put things away in their cases and back to where they are stored after you have finished listening.

Organizing your videos

The same use it or lose it rules apply to videos and DVDs. If you have switched to the newer technology you will appreciate that it takes up much less space. Sell or give away any redundant technology and let go of the clutter.

If you frequently tape from television, make sure you have a system of knowing what is on each tape. It takes only a few minutes to establish, but could save hours of searching and frayed tempers.

USE IT OR LOSE IT: ENTERTAINMENT

By learning what you want from entertainment, you can tailor your music and video collection to fulfil your personal needs. You can let go of outdated memories and make way for new inspirations to nourish your soul.

GOALS

TO CONTROL THE ABUNDANCE OF ENTERTAINMENT IN YOUR HOME BY LETTING GO OF OLD TECHNOLOGY THAT YOU NO LONGER USE AND ITEMS THAT YOU NO LONGER FIND ENTERTAINING. TO ESTABLISH A SYSTEM THAT WILL ENABLE YOU TO KNOW WHAT YOU OWN AND TO FIND IT QUICKLY. TO CONTAIN YOUR ENTERTAINMENT WITHIN EACH ROOM.

BENEFITS

- Make your entertainment truly entertaining by keeping what reflects who you are today.
- Spend less time trying to find what you own and more time relaxing in a clutter-free zone.

TOOLS

- There are many commercial solutions to storing your media. Which one you choose is a matter of personal preference. Try to select an appropriate design to blend into your environment. Look for units that have a capacity slightly larger than your slimmed-down collection. Racks enable you to see titles quickly. Boxes can also be used, but as they have to be opened and closed are a bit more difficult to access.
- Sturdy cardboard box(es) for recycling

METHOD

Our entertainment collections are very personal, providing insight to all the different phases of our life. Music is evocative of memories, and songs often have associations with events in our lives. Replaying past memories too often can leave us in the past. It is important to take a look at who you are now.

1. Think about all the different types of music you enjoy. For the next week, focus on how the music you play makes you feel. Break it down into the following categories:
- Background
- Dancing
- Relaxing
- Singing
- Spiritual
- Stimulating

Next, think about the areas of your home in which you most enjoy those activities.
- Bedroom
- Dining room
- Kitchen
- Sitting room
- Office

This will become the foundation for organizing your music throughout the house.

2. Gather your sources of entertainment from every area of the house and car into one location. This includes all the old tapes and records that may be hiding in the scary places of your home.

3. Put everything away in its protective case. If you have lost the cases, buy new ones: most record shops sell them very inexpensively.

4. Alphabetize all the music by artist, or whatever system you find easiest for accessing your music quickly. If you are doing videos at the same time, alphabetize them by title.

5. Now that you can see what you own, determine to reduce your collection by one-quarter. If you have really been a hoarder, try to reduce the quantity by half. If you don't know how to begin, do the following:
- Remove all items that are broken.
- Remove all seasonal items that are played only on special occasions.
- Remove all items that no longer reflect your taste.
- Remove all duplicates.

- Place the entertainment used only on special occasions in an out-of-the-way location to enable easier access to those used more frequently.

7. Now choose the organizational method that suits your routine. Divide the music by type – classical, rock, jazz, show scores – or by mood, as listed in step 1. The more you are able to understand what role music plays in your life, the more easily you will be able to identify future purchases. You will also find that your music will be more appropriate when listened to in the environment that matches your mood.

This exercise should be undertaken by all members of the household who listen to music in communal areas. It is important to teach your children at a young age to appreciate the value of their videos, music and games by putting things away so they are easy to find.

8. If you find that you have been spending too much money on entertainment, look at the last 10 purchases you made and ask yourself these questions:
- How often have you listened to these 10 CDs since you first purchased them?
- Is there a pattern to your boredom threshold?
- How much money have you spent on entertainment in the last month?
- Do you feel that you have received value from your purchases?

9. Now think about your 10 favourite CDs or tapes and ask yourself these questions:
- How long have you had them in your collection?
- How often do you listen to them?
- Are your top 10 favourites consistent with your current purchases?

10. Use technology to help in your conquest of space. CD writers enable you to download your CD collection to the hard drive of your computer and access your collection whenever you need it. Once you have downloaded, you can recycle your CDs or sell them through second-hand shops. This would enable you to limit the selection you have on display to your current favourites. The initial investment would more than pay for itself by freeing up space throughout your home.

11. Organize your videotapes so that you can tell at a glance what is on each tape:
- Assemble all your recording tapes and stick an adhesive label to the outside. Label each tape with a number.
- Buy a small loose-leaf binder and number the pages, leaving several pages between each number.
- When you record something, write the title on the appropriately numbered page in your notebook. When you tape over the recording, cross off the previous title and write the new title underneath.

ON–GOING PROGRAMME

Make it a point to spend time entertaining, either yourself or a group of friends or family. Remind yourself why you have the music or films you have chosen to keep.

For the next month, monitor your spending patterns on entertainment. Write down all the items you purchase, and focus your attention on how often you listen to the things you buy.

If you find that you are falling back into excessive spending patterns, reduce your budget by 50 per cent. Rather than buying something every time you visit a record shop, enjoy the experience of going in to listen. Buy what you truly enjoy.

Revisit your music storage area in two weeks and review the situation. Is everything organized and in its place? If you find that clutter begins to return, set aside an hour each week to make sure that things are all put away.

If you continue to have problems with clutter in this area, perhaps you use music and entertainment as a form of escape from the present moment. Look at how much time you are spending in these pursuits and if you find that it is too much, try to reduce the amount of time or change your routine to different times and days.

Leisure activities

Letting go of the reminders of leisure activities that you no longer make time for or continue to enjoy is a difficult task. Hobbies and leisure interests represent the person you want to be – more creative, more fit, more interesting. When you confront the junk that has piled up because you no longer have the time or interest for the hobbies connected with it, you must confront the changes in your life that brought about the situation. Understanding why you hold on to the junk can empower you to change your lifestyle and accommodate your interests or let them go.

As you go through the various phases of life, your tastes and interests may change. What you thought was a great game or sport at 20 may not be appropriate at age 40. Your physical condition may limit what you are able to do.

When you marry or move in with a partner, you might abandon solitary hobbies and opt for new activities that can be done as a couple. By holding on to things that you no longer do, you are living in the past. Letting them go allows you to focus your attention on the new things that have entered your life.

The arrival of children may prevent you from finding the time to engage actively in your favourite pastimes. You put things on hold in the hope that you will come back to them when time allows. Keeping reminders of things you are unable to enjoy can lead to resentment and frustration.

Another common reason for letting these things pile up is that many pursuits are costly. The initial enthusiasm for bicycling or playing golf, for example, can fade but the equipment sits hidden away because of the guilt associated with wasting money.

Many people cannot maintain their initial enthusiasm for the duration of a project. Boredom sets in and the project is set aside. It is common to begin another new project before the previous one has been abandoned. In most cases, nothing is completed. By letting go of things you will never finish, you admit to yourself that you are giving up. Not doing something any longer does not necessarily mean that you have lost the desire to do it. Although you haven't pursued the interest in a long time, you might find that you continue to purchase items related to it in the hope that it will re-kindle your enthusiasm or that you will find the time to do it. Your inner self may be trying to tell you something.

The simple answer is that we really do want to have a life that enables us to enjoy things that bring us pleasure. By letting go of the real clutter in your life, you will become more aware of your true inner desires and goals.

Craft projects

Most people who take up craft projects have developed the right side of their brain, which controls the creative side of their personality. Creative people view things differently: they are more visual and tactile. Shopping itself becomes an inspirational event, as virtually anything can stimulate the creative process. However, this can also lead to purchasing more than is required.

Creative people tend to let their inspirations overtake their ability to finish projects, and I am as guilty as anyone of letting creative clutter get out of control in my life. My best friend, whom I met soon after arriving in London, shared my professional background. We had both been knitwear designers and run small businesses. We travelled on many buying adventures, sharing our passion for fabrics and yarns. Over the years, we collected stacks of beautiful materials, far more than we would ever use. We would both begin new projects with enthusiasm, but run out of steam or be inspired by something better, so most things were never completed. It became a longstanding joke between us, and when she was dying, I asked her to become my angel of unfinished projects.

In going through her personal items with her husband, we smiled as we looked at rooms filled with fabrics, knitting paraphernalia and unfinished projects. This experience made me more aware of my habits, and I can now resist the temptation to purchase more than I can complete.

Sports equipment

Health and appearance are very important issues for everyone. They make us confront some of our most complicated feelings about how people view us, and force us to think about the ageing process.

The purchases we make to improve our health and appearance are often made at times when these areas feel threatened. A classic example is when you have gained weight and decide to lose it by purchasing some home exercise equipment or taking up cycling. Ill health may also serve as a wake-up call to begin a programme of fitness and relaxation. In most cases, the equipment lasts longer than the routine. Difficulties associated with letting it go include the necessity of acknowledging that you didn't achieve what you set out to do and guilt about the money you spent. Many families also have reminders of their children's youth in the form of dated and outgrown sports equipment – bicycles, swings, climbing frames and smaller items such as bats and balls. Long after childhood has flown, these items remain as reminders of youth.

USE IT OR LOSE IT: LEISURE EQUIPMENT

If the clutter from activities you no longer pursue is hanging around reminding you that you are not spending enough time on yourself, get to grips with the issues that are preventing you from being who you want to be.

GOALS

TO RID YOUR HOME OF THE CLUTTER ASSOCIATED WITH ACTIVITIES THAT NO LONGER INTEREST YOU. TO ORGANIZE A ROUTINE THAT ALLOWS YOU TO HAVE LEISURE TIME EACH DAY. TO FOCUS YOUR ATTENTION ON TAKING ACTION TO COMPLETE PROJECTS.

BENEFITS

- Spending less money on purchasing things you are unlikely to finish.
- Creating more space for the activities that are relevant to your life at this moment.
- Learning to pursue things that you enjoy.

TOOLS

- Sturdy boxes
- Rubbish bags
- Charity bags
- Labels

METHOD

All household members who have activity-related junk should participate in this project. You should set aside an afternoon to finish the task.

1. Collect all the junk associated with your leisure activities into one space. If larger items are stored in a garage, treat that area separately.

2. Sort everything according to activity – sewing materials in one area, fitness gear in another, and so on.

3. Make a list of all the different hobbies you have started. For each one, think about the following questions.
- How did you initially become interested in the hobby?
- How often did you engage in the activity when you first began?
- Was anything significant happening in your life at the time the hobby began?
- How long did it retain your interest?
- What made you stop?
- Would you like to pursue the activity again?
- What is getting in the way?

Try to gain an understanding of the reasons that you participated in each activity. You may find that they filled mental, physical or emotional needs at the time you began them, and that these needs no longer exist.

4. All the items associated with these activities should be recycled in one way or another. The more costly items are easy to sell through local newspapers; see also the suggestions on page 130.

Schools, hospitals and charity shops accept old games, sports equipment and craft projects and they will stand a better chance of being completed.

5. Of the items remaining that you might use again, prioritize them in order of those that would best suit your current lifestyle. Set aside your top choice and discard all the other items.

6. Now go through all the stuff you have accumulated for your chosen hobby. Bin any items that are broken or useless, such as old paint. Recycle any duplicate materials and any unfinished projects that you have no desire to complete. Keep only those you intend to use straight away.

7. Make a conscious decision to fit this activity into your weekly routine and schedule time in your diary. Focus your attention on what you can complete in the present, and your leisure activities will provide you with personal satisfaction.

ON-GOING PROGRAMME

It takes repeated effort on a consistent basis to develop a habit, good or bad. To get into the habit of making time for the things that make you feel good about yourself, you must incorporate them into your daily routine. Be realistic about your life and set the routine at a pace you can achieve.

During the first month of a new activity, pay attention to how often you stick to your routine. Think about whether the activity brings you pleasure or feels more like a chore. Let go of it if you don't enjoy it. If you start slipping out of the practice, look at the reasons why and make the necessary changes to give you time for your personal development.

Newspapers and magazines

Out-of-control piles of newspapers and magazines are among the most common hotspots in the many homes I have visited. One desperate woman called me when she was ready to confront the fact that her magazines filled an entire bathroom from floor to ceiling, including the bath itself, and she was unable to use the room for its intended purpose.

One of the most obvious problems of being overrun by papers and magazines is that they take up an enormous amount of space, in extreme cases causing physical barriers to doors and rooms. They can also be a fire hazard. Over time, the paper will yellow and disintegrate and become an even greater problem to solve.

When most people are asked why they keep old newspapers and magazines, they usually claim that they refer back to them. In reality, this is not the case.

The situation just requires a bit of discipline. Make it a practice to dispose of daily papers every day and weekend papers by the Sunday night. Old news is just that. Monthly magazines should be around no longer than a month. Check with your local authority for information on recycling and make it a point to dispose of all the household paper each week so it doesn't get out of control.

If you have magazines that you use often for reference, and space is not a problem, keep the issues in order so that you can access them easily when needed. De-junking is an ongoing process, not just a one-time binge. Try to evaluate how you really do use the things that you haven't disposed of, and continue the editing process when you find that they are just sitting around and collecting dust.

If space is a problem, there are several ways around it. Go through the magazines, take out the relevant pages and start your own reference file, keeping separate folders for each topic. The more organized you make your system, the more likely you will be to maintain it. If, after you have downsized, you still don't use the magazines or the files of information, remember to lose them.

Sometimes we have more than physical constraints to worry about. The woman who let magazines take over an entire room, for example, had a problem that was more emotional than physical. Allowing that sort of situation to occur can mean that you are living in the past, so it would be worth taking some time to think about what was going on in your life right before you started letting the newspapers and magazines become a problem. It may take only the realization of the true nature of your problem to enable you to move forward and let go of the past.

Too many subscriptions

Perhaps you have had things on subscription for a long time. Do you really read them when they arrive? Do they reflect your current lifestyle?

By getting rid of things that no longer reflect who you are, you can leave some room for things that reflect who you are now. If you began subscribing to a magazine in your twenties and still get it 10 years later, does it really relate to you now?

Routine purchases

Are you the type of person who has the same routine every day, which includes purchasing newspapers and magazines? If you fit into this category, perhaps it is the actual buying that you really enjoy. This is a cycle that is easily broken by disposing of newspapers before they get taken home and build up.

Going over old ground

Do you find yourself spending lots of time going through old magazines? If so, this suggests you are not feeling connected to the things going on around you at the moment. Reliving the past is important to enable you to learn lessons, but it is then important to let go and move on. You should not rush this process, but gradually reduce your collection to those titles that are most important to you.

USE IT OR LOSE IT:
NEWSPAPERS AND MAGAZINES

For the next week, pay attention to how you purchase your papers and magazines, and when you read them. Looking at why we fall into certain routines enables us to confront the problem and find ways of solving it. Understanding why we do it empowers us to rid ourselves of this negative energy routine. Each member of the household that contributes to the overall problem should participate in this exercise.

GOALS

TO RID YOUR HOME OF ALL UNNECESSARY PAPERS AND TO FIND FUNCTIONAL SPACE FOR KEEPING THOSE THAT YOU USE REGULARLY.

BENEFITS

- Freeing up space in your home and living in the present moment.
- Letting go of the 'old news' will enable you to be more fully aware of what is going on around you.

TOOLS

- Plenty of sturdy boxes to haul off paper for recycling
- Ring binders in which to save reference material
- Rubbish bags for general waste
- Shelving – plan in advance any shelving or additional items that you might require for storing and recycling your papers.

METHOD

1. Think about how many papers or magazines you really need. Look at why you get them. For each item, think about what benefits you derive from it. How much of it do you read? How long do papers and magazines remain in the house without being looked at?

2. Many of the reasons for letting papers pile up are simply a matter of breaking a habit that you may not even realize you have:
- If you have a number of magazine subscriptions, take a positive step and cancel any that no longer suit your lifestyle. As an added incentive, think about how much money you spend on these items you never use. What would you rather spend the money on?
- If you buy newspapers on a daily basis as part of your routine, try spending the same amount of time making fewer purchases. If you read while you are on public transport, see if you can finish your selection by the end of your journey and dispose of it before you

get home. It is often the case that people take papers home and never finish them, so the cycle starts again.

• If you tend to go over old magazines, begin by saying to yourself that you are going to reduce your collection by half, and then organize them so that each title is in its own pile. You may well be reading the same information about the same people and places in different magazines, so try to pick the title you like best and let go of the rest. Go through this process in each subject area (fashion, interiors, etc.) until you are able to reduce the number of magazines in your home.

3. Dispose of all the excess paper you have accumulated in your life. In order to break your old routines, try to pick a new area in which to keep only current paperwork. If possible, also try to select a new place for the recycling if that is a clutter hotspot. Moving things around changes the flow of energy in a room, and you might just come across the perfect places that make the job easier.

4. Evaluate how you feel about the changes you have made. Do they change the appearance of the room? Is it physically easier to get around? Are you able to locate things more quickly? Do you spend more time in the room? Do you miss any of the items you disposed of?

ON-GOING PROGRAMME
Revisit this clutter hotspot in one month's time. If you find that you are falling back into old patterns, start the process again and revisit the spot in two weeks' time. Pay attention to the patterns and change your routine.

Paperwork

Excess paperwork is the single biggest contributor to cluttered environments in homes and offices. We accumulate so many papers each day that systems have to be in place to deal with them or they start to overtake us and affect our efficiency. Not dealing with paperwork immediately impinges on our space, time, money and health. These are good enough reasons to take charge, clear out excess papers and get on top of the situation.

When offices become out of control, the paper stacks up. When paper becomes a problem at home, it spreads out and stacks up. The more space that's available, the more paper accumulates.

Papers tend to congregate most often on the first available surface that you stop at when you get home. Hallways, kitchens and bedrooms are paperwork hotspots. In all the homes we visited for the TV series, we found that papers had taken over every available work surface, preventing the families from using the rooms for their intended purpose. In one home we even found papers stacked on top of the cooker, which is a frightening fire hazard. When paper clutter puts your family and possessions at risk, it is time to take action.

Out-of-control paperwork is also a constant reminder that you are not dealing with many issues in your life. Every day that you are faced with lots of unfinished business means that you are more likely to feel that you are not accomplishing your goals in life. Paying a bill or finding a relevant bit of information when you need it becomes a laborious and time-consuming chore. Rather than taking five minutes to action when it arrives, the process can take hours. What could be a simple chore now becomes a drudgery that requires far more energy to complete and leaves you drained in the process.

Things often get lost, making you feel out of control. You must then spend time making phone calls to ask for even more paper to enter your life. Bills can get overlooked and you may find that you fail to turn up at an important event. All these situations create tension and stress. Health problems often follow.

One of the biggest obstacles to confronting your piles of paperwork is not knowing what papers you should keep. You are, in fact, legally required to produce certain documents on demand, such as licences and insurance certificates. Other essential documents prove ownership of your most important possessions. These include the deeds to your home and share certificates. It is advisable to keep the originals of these documents in either a fireproof container or with your solicitor. Keep photocopies for your own files so that the information is readily accessible when you require it.

The law requires you to keep all your tax documentation for seven years. This means that everything related to your business activities and personal income, such as bank statements, receipts, credit card bills, invoices and dividend statements must be kept in a safe place. Armed with the knowledge of what you need to keep, it is easy to establish systems that will help you organize your paperwork as you require. Anything that doesn't fall in the 'essential' category can be released so that you can reclaim all your living space for living in.

CASE STUDY:

One of our contributor's homes was overrun with paperwork. They were both professional journalists employed outside the home who each felt a need to have their own office to accommodate their expanding collection of files and paperwork.

They lived in a former council house that had six rooms, and were using two of those rooms for offices. Their paperwork completely filled one room and spilled into the other, leaving both rooms difficult to work in.

They both collected all the magazines with their articles and held on to piles and piles of junk mail, old envelopes and outdated files that were no longer required or relevant.

By getting rid of their excess paperwork and limiting what they collected of their published works (only the article rather than the entire magazine), they were able to work from one tidy, professional office with room enough to house both of their filing systems comfortably.

The remaining room was converted into a library and reading room, creating more useable space in their home. We crushed or recycled 95 bags of rubbish, mostly comprised of old and unnecessary papers.

USE IT OR LOSE IT: PAPERWORK

This project will require you to dedicate as much time as it takes to wade through all the piles of paper in your house. Many documents are difficult to replace, so it is essential to deal with each piece of paper. The end result will be dramatic and will release an enormous weight from your mind.

GOALS   **TO RID ALL AREAS OF YOUR HOME OF ALL UNNECESSARY FILES AND PAPERS. TO DEVELOP A FILING SYSTEM FOR ALL YOUR DIFFERENT TYPES OF PAPERWORK. TO PUT A ROUTINE IN PLACE SO THAT YOU CAN ACTION CORRESPONDENCE WHEN IT ARRIVES.**

BENEFITS
- Dealing with your financial matters on a regular basis will help you to protect your credit rating and save you money on late credit payments.
- Letting go of papers relating to traumatic events in your life can enable you to let go of the past and live in the present moment.
- Learning to take action when a situation occurs enables you to feel more in control of your day-to-day routines and more optimistic about life.

TOOLS   Depending on your circumstances, the amount of filing space required will vary. If you work from home, you will probably need to have at least one filing cabinet to hold your relevant information.
- Sturdy cardboard boxes with lids
  (get more than you think you will require)
- Heavy-duty rubbish bags
- Adhesive labels
- Marker pens
- Rubber bands
- Wallet folders
- Suspension files (for filing cabinet)
- Lever arch files or large ring binders
- Accordion file (numbered 1–31 for the days of the month)
- In/Out trays
- Diary
- Hole punch
- Staples

METHOD

1. Over the next week, keep notes on the types of paper that enter the house and what you do with each type. Pay attention to the following documents:
- Junk mail
- Bank/credit card statements
- Receipts
- Bills
- Business cards/telephone numbers
- Social correspondence
- Office work
- Guarantees/Appliance manuals
- Children's schoolwork
- Medical records

2. Now look at your current methods of dealing with the following situations:
- Paying bills
- Entering commitments in your diary
- Writing letters
- Checking bank/credit card statements
- Doing expense reports (if required)

3. Look at the results of steps 1 and 2 and try to determine if you have developed any type of routine to address each task. Answer the following questions:
- How often do you perform this task?
- Do you always sit in the same location when performing this task?
- Do you keep the papers relating to this task in the same location?
- What do you do with the papers when you have completed the task?

Now that you have become more aware of how you currently deal with your papers, it will be easier to understand where the best place is to keep them.

4. Tackle your paper mountain in one go, no matter how painstaking the process may be. Clear a large space and gather all your papers in this one location. This includes old documents that may be boxed and stored in the loft or garage.

5. Your filing cabinet, or whatever filing system you use on a day-to-day basis, should contain documents for only the last two years. Anything older should be boxed, clearly labelled and put in safe, dry storage space, such as a loft or cupboard.

6. Create files for the most usual types of correspondence you receive. These should include individual files for each bank account, credit card and bill that you receive on a regular basis.

7. Next, create files for permanent documents, such as instruction manuals, guarantees, or take-away menus.

8. Now create files for all the other paper that is relevant to your life. For example, you might need files for paperwork about your children, or for information relating to special projects. These files should be reviewed monthly to update or discard.

9. Starting with your more recent papers, sort them into piles that correspond with all the files you have set up. As you do this, you will probably find a good deal of rubbish and outdated information. Be ruthless and lighten the load.

10. Outstanding bills should be placed in the accordion file. Make time to check them as errors can and do occur. Write out the cheque and put it in the envelope with the tear-off slip of the bill. Stamp and date the outside of the envelope with the date it needs to posted, not the date it is due. Place the envelope in the appropriate date of the file. Place the retained part of the bill in the appropriate folder of your filing system.
   If you pay your bills by direct debit, keep a statement pending file of bils that need to be referenced to bank statements. Reference the statement with the payment detail reference from the bank statement and file chronologically.

11. Place personal letters or other correspondence in your in-tray to action within the week. Writing is a great way to take action and stay connected to the moment.

12. Transfer all addresses, phone numbers or diary events you have collected on loose bits of paper into the relevant diary, address book or computer. Get rid of the scraps of paper. Remember to do this exercise at regular intervals in the future.

13. If you keep business cards, place them in an appropriate file or box. (I find it easier to transfer them into a computer or diary.)

14. Make the necessary notes on any receipts that you are required to keep for tax purposes. To prevent them from getting lost, tape or staple them to sheets of A4. If you have to surrender them to reclaim expenses, photocopy the sheets for your records.

15. Keep all your tax documents for each year in a sturdy box with a lid. Be sure to label the outside with the relevant tax period. You must keep your records for seven years. Dispose of any records that are no longer required.

ON–GOING PROGRAMME

Make the decision to deal with paperwork every day as it enters your life. Dispose of junk mail immediately.

Check bank statements and credit card bills as soon as they arrive. If you find an error, it is easier to resolve if dealt with promptly.

Prepare your payment as described in step 10 and immediately file the statement.

Deal with any receipts while they are fresh in your mind. Make notes on them of the date and reason for purchase, and fill out any necessary expense forms on a regular basis. Make it a rule to deal with travel expenses on the day you return as a means of finishing the project.

Limit the amount of children's work that you hang in your house as it rapidly becomes messy. Confine the work to their bedrooms and one communal room in the house.

Revisit your paper clutter hotspots in two weeks. If you find that papers are beginning to pile up again, see if they relate to a particular area of your life. Focus your attention on what might be causing the neglect and use the problem-solving and goal-setting techniques in Chapter 2 to arrive at a solution. Continue monitoring your progress to make sure that you don't fall into old habits.

Sentimental items

Some of the most common sentimental items that we are most reluctant to give away are old photographs and personal letters and cards. By taking an objective view, you may find that some of the former emotional attachments that you held for these objects no longer exists, and you can easily let go of them.

A house truly becomes a home when there are objects that convey the history of the people living in it. However, those who hoard sentimental items and seem to be stuck in the past must find the strength to let go of these past emotions to move on in their lives. The inability to confront past situations, as in the case study on pages 108–9, often leads to serious illness.

If you have had many physical problems, it would be worth looking back to when they first started. When you establish the dates, look at the two-year period leading up to it. What was happening in your life at the time? Perhaps there was something unpleasant that you have chosen to block out, even if it did not seem traumatic at the time. Releasing this past trauma will help to release the blockage and can make you feel better.

Begin by clearing sentimental possessions dating from the time the trauma may have occurred. Bring them out of your unopened boxes and confront what you find. Look in all your drawers and other hiding places around the house, and form the intention that you will let go of things relating to the unhappy situation. Only then will you be able to let the feelings go. Enlist the support of close friends and family, or seek professional help if you feel unable to confront the situation on your own.

Photographs

Few families maintain rigid rules about putting photographs in albums or proper storage containers, so they often take over boxes and drawers throughout the house. When not stored properly, they quickly deteriorate and just take up space.

It is lovely to keep photographs of your family history for future generations, but they serve little purpose if they are just collecting dust somewhere. Frame the most meaningful photographs and hang them somewhere they can be appreciated.

Try to learn to disciminate between good and average photographs and keep only the best. Immediately discard any that are out of focus or of poor quality. Send the remaining ones to family or friends or throw them away. This should help significantly in reducing the number you store.

If you tend to take lots of photographs but never refer back to them, take less film when you next use your camera. Try to compose each shot rather than shooting randomly. It saves money and space.

Try to put in albums all photographs that you plan to keep. Capture the moment but don't hold on to every minor detail. Let your imagination fill in the blanks. Photo albums make wonderful gifts for family, so start planning what to do with your photographs as soon as you've had them developed.

Personal letters and cards

In the same case study on pages 108–9, the mother admitted that she kept old cards because it reminded her that people cared about her. She would look at them when she was feeling particularly low.

We hold on to old words as a reminder of who we were at that time. Releasing them allows us not to play the same role again in another situation.

Go through all your places that you keep your personal correspondence and rid yourself of those items that may be associated with unpleasant memories or no longer have any meaning to you. Try to make it a point of disposing of all but the most meaningful cards and letters no later than several weeks after the event. Keeping them on display makes them a dust trap and they rarely get looked at after they are received.

USE IT OR LOSE IT: SENTIMENTAL ITEMS

If you find yourself incapacitated by past emotions that you are unable to release, look at the unpleasant reminders of that past so that you can clear the air and become connected to the present.

GOALS

TO CLEAR AWAY ALL SENTIMENTAL OBJECTS BOTH ON DISPLAY AND IN STORAGE THAT MAY BE CAUSING EMOTIONAL BLOCKAGES TO PHYSICAL WELL-BEING.

BENEFITS

- Getting rid of sentimental clutter will lighten your load of junk and make more space in your home and life for what is relevant at the moment.
- Understanding how important it is to confront emotional situations when they occur rather than holding on to the physical junk associated with them will help you to make a new start.

TOOLS

- Sturdy boxes
- Newspaper
- Photo albums
- Rubbish bags for excess paper and charity-shop donations

METHOD

1. Seek out the sentimental clutter in your home. The easiest approach is to do it on a room-by-room basis, going through every nook and cranny to list all potential items that you are willing to let go.

2. Determine the best way to dispose of each item. Think of three situations that you have held on to, but are now willing to let go. Write them down, beginning with the least emotional situation first. For each situation, think about where you feel the emotion in your body. Imagine that there is a cloud in the area of the emotion, then release your emotions from that situation into the cloud. Try to think of the cloud getting lighter in colour and rising until you are able to raise it over your head. Just as real clouds lift and the weather improves, so clouds of emotion can be lifted and depression eased. Release all of the physical matter relating to these situations.

- Offer items you no longer use to your relatives or friends. As evidenced by the many people who attend car boot sales, one person's junk is another's treasure. Do not feel embarrassed by what you own. If possible, get people to take items away as soon as they have accepted them.

- Carefully wrap and box all breakables to dispose of through a car boot sale, auction house or charity shop. (See pages 126–30 for some tips on how to make the most money from these items. On pages 112–25 you will also find hints on how to clean valuable items that you may have re-discovered.) Label the outside of each box so you can quickly see what's in it.
- Any items that are not damaged can be given away to local charity shops. Paper should be sent for recycling, and all other rubbish disposed of immediately.
- Items of value that are no longer used can be disposed of in many ways. See Chapter 5 to find ways of deciding whether something is valuable and the best means of selling it.
- If you are holding on to furniture in order to pass it on to members of your family, why not ask if they would like to have it now? This serves two purposes: it clears your space and allows the recipient to decide whether they would like to own it.
- Now is a good time to assess things you have inherited but don't appreciate. Decide to sell them and put the money towards something that will have more meaning to you as you are currently living.

3. Make a list of sentimental items you wish to keep. Examine your reasons for keeping them. Are they well looked after? Are they in a place in your home that enables you to enjoy them? Use them or lose them.

ON−GOING PROGRAMME

Over the next month, review all the things that have entered your home.
    Assess how you dealt with photographs during this four-week period. Were you able to dispose of those that were not worth keeping? Did you store the remainder in an organized way?
    How long did you hold on to personal correspondence? If you continue to hold on to these things, think about your reasons. Determine to let go of 50 per cent of the new items you have kept.
    Did you receive any gifts that you will not use? Make a list of what you would use, and offer them as suggestions when asked in future what you would like.
    Continue to be aware of the emotional content of your possessions.

Toys and children's clothing

Holding on to toys and outgrown clothing can be a problem for many families as their children start to get older. There are several issues that must be dealt with. The first is to look at why you feel the need to keep these items; the second is to examine your buying patterns; and the third is to evaluate your storage systems for them.

Holding on to toys and outgrown clothing can be a problem for many families as their children start to get older. There are several issues that must be dealt with. The first is to look at why you feel the need to keep these items; the second is to examine your buying patterns; and the third is to evaluate your storage systems for them.

A common reason for holding on to children's memorabilia is because you find it difficult to let your children grow up. You are the centre of their infant universe, but as they start to formulate their own ideas and opinions from their interaction with the world, your influence on them begins to lessen. By holding on to their toys, you may be trying to hold on to a time in your life when you felt younger and more in control. You may also be trying to keep your children young and innocent.

In some cases, letting go of children's toys means that you are acknowledging to yourself that you will not be having more children. This may be difficult to accept: however, holding on to these reminders prevents you from moving on to new chapters in your life.

All parents want the best for their children and will often sacrifice their own material desires to make sure their kids have everything they need. What you must determine is how much of what your children own is what they need as opposed to what they want. There may be items that your children never play with, perhaps because you bought them for yourself.

Taking the time to assess why you buy so much is an integral part of getting to the bottom of your clutter problems. In family situations, you lead by example, so your buying habits are likely to form the foundation for how your children perceive the value of money. Do you repeat habits you learned as a child?

Buying from guilt is something else that will be familiar to most adults with busy lives. As more and more families are made up of two working parents, the need or desire to pursue careers can lead to toys being bought as compensation for not being able to spend more time with the children.

Toys are often given to elicit good behaviour or, in some circumstances, to stop bad behaviour. We have all witnessed or experienced situations where children misbehave in shops and the parent buys the child a toy rather than having a scene.

Playing with toys is an integral part of your child's development, stimulating their imagination and creativity. Choosing the right toys to help your child reach their maximum potential is an enormous responsibility. Make sure that you are buying toys suited to the age of your child. They are not always something that your child grows into. Buying toys that are too old for the current stage of development can be dangerous and frustrating.

It is important to teach your children at a young age that they must value and look after things. When toys begin to spread throughout the house, it is necessary to establish a system that teaches your child to put things away in their place.

Letting go can feel good

My stepdaughters Alison and Emma, aged 22 and 25, respectively, told me a story that happened several years ago when their mother decided to downsize her house after her husband passed away.

Both girls had moved in with my husband and me when their education and jobs were closer to where we live, but they still maintained bedrooms in their old house. All the things from their rooms and the loft would not fit into their mother's new house, so she offered them anything they wanted from their old home, but stipulated that it all had to be gone by the next day.

While going through their things in the loft, they came across a box of old dolls and soft toys that had provided them with lovely times when they were children. They reminisced about growing up and then packed up what they truly treasured. They donated the remaining items to their local charity shop.

Several days later, they were walking down the high street and saw a little girl coming out of the charity shop with one of their dolls, which was wearing a distinctive dress they had made. Although it had been emotional letting go of their childhood memories, seeing a little girl cuddling the doll felt far better than letting it sit in a box in the loft. This is a good lesson that we can all learn from, especially when there are so many good causes that need items for children.

USE IT OR LOSE IT:
TOYS AND CHILDREN'S CLOTHES

If you find that children's toys and clothing are out of control, it is time to take stock and teach some lessons about the value of money. Letting go of who your children were when they were infants can help you to see who they are at this moment.

GOALS
TO RECYCLE ALL TOYS AND CLOTHING THAT ARE NO LONGER USED BY YOUR CHILDREN. TO TEACH YOUR CHILDREN THAT ALL THINGS MUST BE LOOKED AFTER. TO UNDERSTAND WHAT ROLE TOYS PLAY IN YOUR CHILDREN'S LIVES.

BENEFITS
• Fewer toys and less clutter spread throughout the house.

TOOLS
• Sturdy cardboard boxes or plastic crates
• Large labels

METHOD
1. Observe the toys that your children play with most often.
Try to focus your attention on the following points:
• What type of toy do they play with most often?
• Does the balance of their toys reflect the types of toys they like?
• What toys hold their attention for the longest time?
• Are there some toys that they never play with at all?
• Are their toys balanced between action toys and creative toys?
• Do they play with different toys when they are with their friends?
• Do they have special toys they take with them to school?
• Do they sleep with any special toys?
• Are they playing with toys for their age group?

2. Take away the toys that are never played with or that have been outgrown. It is a good time to explain to your children that they are getting bigger, and there are many younger children who could use their toys. They can be given to local playgroups, hospitals and charity shops. Recognize that what your child no longer requires will give endless pleasure to another child.

3. Plan to spend several hours with your children sorting out the toys in the house so that they are better able to find things on their own. The best way to do this is to make it a fun project.

Colour coding is a good way to get children to put things away. Get some sturdy cardboard boxes of uniform size and paint each one a different colour. On the outside of each box, ask your child to draw a picture of what belongs inside. Teach them to sort out their toys and keep the right one inside each box. By making them accountable for their possessions at an early age, they will learn to look after things to make them last.

If your children are older, plastic crates may be a more suitable method of storing their equipment. Make sure that whatever systems you put in place are physically accessible to your children. This means that things should be easy to open and placed at the right height to enable your child to use it on their own.

4. Make a plan to have a major clear-out of all toys scattered throughout the house. It is important to try to get your children to put away all toys that they wish to keep and gather all the rest for your favourite charity. Try to develop a routine that gets them into the habit of putting their toys away each evening prior to bedtime. As your children begin to understand their routine, begin to take away any toys that are not put away.

5. Become more aware of how and what you purchase for your children. Keep track of all your purchases for the next four weeks. Note what made you decide to buy – a special event, a special request from a child, guilt, or a liking for something cute. See how long the toy keeps your children's attention and whether they value it.

ON–GOING PROGRAMME

In order to teach your children that they can't have everything they want, think about establishing a system whereby for every new toy received, they must give away something old. This is a great way to teach them to appreciate what they receive.

Monitor the types of toys that keep your children occupied and intellectually stimulated so that you will learn the best types of toys to purchase.

Try to plan purchases rather than buy them on the spur of the moment. Involve your children in the process by creating a reward system that encourages good behaviour.

Wardrobe

In all my years of looking through people's wardrobes, I have only ever met a handful of individuals who used everything they owned. I hate to admit it, but they were mostly men, and they were all frequent travellers, which helped them to develop a system of picking only necessary items. One spent several months a year sailing and learned to live with what he could pack in two suitcases. It is surprising how little we really need to survive.

Unfortunately, the wardrobe seems to be the area of life in which everyone is a hoarder. Most of us wear the same 20 per cent of our clothes most of the time. The remainder is worn occasionally or, more commonly, not at all. For many people, just being able to see what they own is a challenge.

There is a whole host of reasons for why we hold on to clothes. And there are just as many reasons for why we feel the need to keep buying them. What you wear and how you present yourself to the world reveal how you view yourself. What does your clothing say about you?

The best way to come to grips with your wardrobe is to decide why your clothing seems to be such an important part of your life. Looking at the reasons why you hold on to old clothes or continue to purchase things that you do not need will help you to break the negative energy pattern. Perhaps looking at some common reasons that people hold on to old clothing will also enable you to have a more realistic approach to what you need.

It is also important to look at the reasons why you shop. We all have to do some sort of shopping to get the basics we need to survive. Excessive shopping, however, is often an escape from things in your life that are bothering you. Looking at your shopping habits can give you insight to what is at the root of the problem. Common reasons for excessive shopping include regarding it as a social or leisure activity, an escape from a troubling situation or place, and a way of feeling in control.

CASE STUDY: COMPULSIVE ABOUT CLOTHES

Many of the issues that this family faced are common to those who find controlling their wardrobe a difficult task.

The family consists of four members – a husband and wife in their late fifties and two children in their mid-twenties. Both children had left home, and as more space became available, the couple continued to buy or bring things into the home until most surfaces were covered in junk. The wife had been very prominent in the community and was a head teacher until illness (two bouts of cancer) forced her retirement in 1994.

The husband had been made redundant and started his own business looking after properties in the village. When she no longer had work to fill her day, shopping became a replacement activity, filling the void of social interaction and giving her the feeling of control that was not being experienced in other areas of her life. He was often asked by his clients to clear away their unwanted junk. Rather than seeing it go to waste, he would take it home in the hope that it would get recycled. The sheer volume of things in the house made it impossible to know where to begin the clearance.

Clutter had taken over their lives, covering every surface in most of the rooms with piles of junk. Items that belonged in the garage began creeping indoors, and the rooms no longer functioned as they were intended. Papers were stacked on top of the cooker and it was clear that things had got out of control.

The worst area was the spacious master bedroom, which contained a very large walk-in wardrobe adjoined by what was supposed to be an en-suite bathroom. It had been plumbed and ready to fit for 20 years, but had been filled instead with clothes and old papers dating back to when the house was first built. A medium-sized wardrobe was on the opposite side of the room, with two chests of drawers on the opposite wall. A bookshelf that couldn't cope with all the books in the room was behind the door. The bed was opposite a wall of windows and had a bedside table on each side.

The room was littered with piles of clothes, papers and books, old cosmetics, jewellery and shoes. The door to the bedroom had not shut in years, and the wardrobes were so stuffed with clothes that you could not walk inside or close the doors. Piles of clothes were stacked under the windows and on the floor, they hung over the hallway railings and covered every surface in the guest room and daughter's bedroom.

The moment of awakening came when the daughter needed to move back home and was unable to unpack for weeks because the parents' clothing took over her space. When faced with all their possessions laid out on the lawn, the couple were able to see the extent of the problem. They let go of many years' worth of emotional and material attachment, leaving them with what they needed. Some 35 bin bags went to charity. A further 15 were either recycled or compacted. Almost 70 per cent of the things they owned had little relevance to their lives and they were able to let them go. The house felt lighter and more energetic. The couple began to plan for the future rather than living in the past.

USE IT OR LOSE IT: CLOTHING

If you find that you don't know what you own, or compulsively buy clothing that you don't need and don't wear, put your life on the lawn and come to grips with your outward appearance to the world.

GOALS
TO GO THROUGH YOUR WARDROBE AND KEEP ONLY WHAT YOU NEED AND TO SEE IF YOUR WARDROBE TRULY REFLECTS YOUR CURRENT LIFESTYLE.

BENEFITS
- Spend less money on clothing and save time getting ready.
- Start a new pattern to know what you need rather than want.
- Let go of old lifestyles and get your wardrobe to work for you.

TOOLS
- Heavy-duty rubbish bags
- Luggage tags
- Breathable storage containers
- Lavender or cedar (optional)
- Charity bags
- Notebook

METHOD
One of the main reasons that people with excessive clothing continue buying is that they do not know what they currently own. This is usually because things are poorly organized and sometimes scattered throughout the house. When you are able to have everything in one place you can see more clearly what you own and come to understand your buying patterns.

1. Gather your clothing from all areas of your house into one room. This includes everything you have packed away in storage.

2. Separate your clothing into seasons. Only the current season should be in your wardrobe.

3. Sort your clothing by categories – shirts, trousers, suits, etc. – and hang them in the wardrobe, short things at one end, longer things at the other end.

4. Now sort them by colour.

5. Sort your folded clothing, such as T-shirts and underwear, in the same way, and do the same with your shoes, belts and accessories.

6. Go through your out-of-season clothing and have a good purge before putting them away.
- Anything that is ripped or stained and can't be repaired should be disposed of immediately.
- Give to friends, charity anything that you haven't worn in the past year.
- Admit you are human and make mistakes. Let them go and move on.

7. It is most important to launder or dry clean everything you store. This will preserve the life of your clothing and make it ready to wear when you bring it out next season. To help keep the moths away, try using cedar or lavender products. They also help to keep your clothes smelling fresh.

8. Remove the plastic bags from your dry-cleaning. They do not allow your clothes to breathe and can discolour lighter shades and fabrics. Try to find natural-fibre bags, such as cotton canvas, or use cardboard boxes; both will allow your things to breathe. Make sure you choose a damp proof location, preferably out of extreme heat or sun.

9. Clearly label the outside of the box or bag with tags identifying the contents. This saves time in fruitless searches.

10. Identify a place in the house where you can store all your bags together. (Under the bed, in the loft or under the stairs are frequently used places.) This allows you to control what you have and decide what new items may be needed to complement your existing wardrobe.

Now take a good look at the items in your current wardrobe. Having sorted them by type, colour and size, you can clearly see the individual parts that make up the whole. Write down the excesses and the things that are missing. Rather than repeating past mistakes or continuing to duplicate the same items, look at what you can purchase to complement your existing wardrobe. Make a list and buy only from that list when you go shopping. Look at the things you don't have enough of and target the things you need. Good planning and staying in control of the situation will save money, time and space.

In analyzing your wardrobe, look for the following patterns:
- Do you buy things that are all the same colour?
- Do you buy the same things over and over again?
- Do you wear some items more often than others?
  If so, what is it about them that makes them special?
- Do you have work clothing that no longer reflects your work situation?
- Does your wardrobe reflect the balance of activities in your life?
- Do you have items in your wardrobe that you have never worn?
- Does all your clothing fit you?

12. Decide that you will reduce the 80 per cent of your wardrobe that you never wear or wear only occasionally by half.

13. Let go of all the items you feel guilty about – things you can't fit into, things you never wear, or gifts that don't really suit you.

Money is also a major contributor to guilt. By addressing how much money you spend on clothing you never wear, you can spend more freely in other areas of your life.

14. Stop the cycle of impulse buying by paying closer attention to what you purchase.

15. Dispose of all items of clothing that no longer reflect your lifestyle. If you have changed careers, let go of the old and make way for what you need.

Do the same for shoes, accessories and folded clothing.

ON–GOING
PROGRAMME

Continue to refine and edit your wardrobe.
   Write down what type of clothing you need each day for the next week. Look at what other sorts of event you may go to over a month and decide what type of clothing is required. Plan your wardrobe around how many changes of clothing you require and what type of clothing serves most functions in your life.
   Rather than buying many cheap items, select fewer things of better quality: they will last longer.
   Each time you purchase something new, give something away. Try to reduce your wardrobe to the most manageable amount for your lifestyle.

Scary places

Just as many of our possessions seem to multiply before our eyes, so scary places within our homes seem to attract the clutter like a magnet. These hiding places might make things look tidy on the outside, but the clutter still exists. Like emotions that can stay buried deep inside us if we don't deal with them when they occur, our scary places often contain physical reminders of the most emotional events in our lives. Unless we let go of the physical manifestation of the event, we are unlikely to be able to let go of our buried emotions.

Scary places are not necessarily packed with emotional litter. They can also represent a life that doesn't seem to allow time for a good cleaning routine. These are time-management issues that require you to take more control in planning how to tackle each of the chores around the house. The kitchen is a classic scary place in many homes. By not scheduling a time to go through your storage areas, food may go out of date and get wasted. This is also unhygienic and can be harmful to your health.

Geography is also a major contributor to the scary places in your house. Clutter is most likely to get dumped or hidden in the places that you pass by most often. Hallways are almost always a clutter trap and cupboards under the stairs frequently seem to get out of control. The habit of using these places as dumping grounds can be broken by utilizing each space for the most appropriate purpose.

By targeting what items should be stored in each location, you will know what you own and be able to find it when you need it. Divide and conquer has always been the best strategy for space planning. Assign everything a place in your home and you will keep your clutter at bay.

Airing cupboards

Few people use airing cupboards for their intended purpose – to air laundry items that are slightly damp. Most families use them for storage. Bedlinen, towels, blankets and duvets are tightly packed inside, making it difficult ever to find anything that matches without the lot tumbling down. Best sets of sheets and towels can be so thoroughly buried that they never get used.

It's well known that many people hide jewellery and money in the airing cupboard, but burglars know this and often make it their first port of call.

Airing cupboards are typically located near a bathroom, as they often house the hot-water tank. The awkward spaces around the tank tend to become traps for soft furnishings or clothing which are easy to pile high and can be made to fit into irregular shapes.

The ideal airing cupboard should have slatted shelves, and holes at the top and bottom of the door to provide a steady flow of air around the cupboard. Ideally, it should store items that are used often, to prevent things such as towels and sheets, from getting too dry. It is also a good place to allow your towels to dry after bathing.

Bedding

Blankets and duvets are the biggest problem in airing cupboards. As times have changed, blankets have become a thing of the past, but many people hang on to them. The first step in sorting out your airing cupboard is to bin these relics.

Take a good look at all the duvets stored in the cupboard. Many people keep different weights for seasonal changes but never bother to swap them over. Look back at what you've used over the last 12 months and dispose of anything that hasn't moved during that time.

Towels

Towels can be a big problem throughout the house. They are bulky to store, are used daily, frequently get dumped on the floor after use and seem to require constant laundering. Too often they seem to hang around when they are old and threadbare.

The easiest way of getting to grips with your towel clutter is first to bin any towels that are ripped or permanently stained. Now look at your remaining towels and divide them by the number of people who use them. This should be each person's weekly ration of towels and should be kept in their rooms to look after. All those able to wash their own clothing should be responsible for their towels.

Bedlinen

Most people are creatures of habit and get into the routine of using the same sheets each week after laundering. It can be surprising how many sets of sheets we actually keep. A good way to edit is to separate the bottom sheets from top sheets, and to put pillowcases and duvet covers into individual piles. Store complete sets together to avoid wasting time trying to match items each time you need them. Any other linen that has not been used in the last six months gets put in the bin.

Other junk

The use of an airing cupboard is so clear cut that anything other than the items discussed above must go. All the remaining junk should be sorted, condensed and put into use in its proper place.

Improvements

- Screw hooks into suitable places inside the cupboard so that you can hang used bathroom towels up to dry. Using towels more than once can dramatically cut down on your laundry time.
- If space permits, install a hanging rail to dry shirts. By gently pulling the shirts into shape after they have been washed and hanging them in the airing cupboard you can cut down on your ironing time.
- If possible, keep one or two shelves free for items, such as jumpers, that need to be dried flat. You might want to place a cloth over the slats to prevent the garment from marking.
- Make it a point to use your linens in rotation. By starting with the item at the bottom of the pile, you will always keep things fresh.
- Hang some cedar or lavender in the airing cupboard to keep away moths.

Bathroom

The bathroom is one of the most personal rooms in the house. It says a lot about your hygiene and, most importantly, how you present yourself to the world outside. The state of your bathroom reflects your current state of your mind.

Daily personal hygiene routines are often determined by the amount of time you allow yourself to undertake them. If you are constantly rushed, the result will be clutter and chaos. This is not the best way to begin each day. Allow yourself extra time in the morning to get yourself off to the best start. This could mean changing your bedtime routines.

Focus your attention on the details in the bathroom. Make it a point to replace caps every time you use a product in there. Things like perfume will evaporate and change if the cap is left off, medicinal solutions will become contaminated, and shower bottles can spill, which is both dangerous and wasteful.

Replace all the essentials as soon as they run out, and be sure to dispose of the finished product immediately. You will be surprised how many empty bottles accumulate in scary places.

Assess whether you are able to use your space efficiently for each part of your daily hygienic routine. Look at the common clutter problems discussed below and apply the ideas to your own bathroom.

Towels

Towels are usually the biggest cause of clutter in a bathroom. Their bulk in a limited space can quickly get out of control. Make it a practice to hang towels up after use: they will dry more quickly and stay fresher longer. Keep only the towels that you use on a daily basis on a towel rail or hook. All other towels should be neatly folded and stored in an airing cupboard or high-level cupboard storage if available.

Laundry

Many people with limited space manage to squeeze a washing-machine into their bathroom, or use it to store their laundry basket for dirty clothes. This obviously compounds bathroom problems with those of the utility room. See the helpful hints on pages 100–1 to help you simplify your laundry clutter zone. Make it a point, however, always to keep dirty clothing off the floor and in the laundry basket. Not doing so is sheer laziness.

Toiletries

Make-up is a purchase that many women find unable to resist. The idea that you are able to enhance your appearance with a particular product surrounds you wherever you look. Look at all the fashion and beauty magazines on the market and you will see that beauty is big business.

Focusing your attention on how and why you purchase cosmetics can help you to lose the things you never use and begin to streamline your space and purchases. There is one golden rule for make-up clutter: use it up in six months or lose it.

Cosmetics come into contact with your fingers and can become unhygienic. Other products may begin to change colour or dry out. Perhaps some of your make-up choices were simply wrong for you. Whatever the case, don't hang on to stuff you no longer use.

Medicines

Make it a rule to throw away all redundant medication, but do make sure you do so safely. Pour liquids down the drain, and return tablets to the chemist for safe disposal. Letting go of medicines symbolically releases the illness.

Reading materials

The bathroom is also a collecting point for newspapers, magazines and books. Remove all dated materials immediately. Old news is old news anywhere in the house.

Improvements

- The bathroom is often the smallest room in the house, so it is essential to use the space efficiently.
- There are many clever storage solutions available to maximize small spaces. Wall space is often wasted in bathrooms, so look for free-standing narrow cupboards that fit between units, or hang cupboards above them. These are ideal places to stack towels and keep personal items that you don't want on display.
- Sort all your products according to how you use them and put them in baskets or plastic containers to maximize space on the sink top or in a cupboard. Being organized will make all your bathroom chores take less time.

Garages and sheds

At the risk of appearing sexist, in my experience, garages and sheds are scary places created mostly by men. They are often bolt-holes where they can spend time alone and pursue their own interests.

During a recent visit to the home of one of our contributors, I had a quick peek inside their garage and shed and found a positive jumble sale. The contents included a 1973 Mini Cooper, seven bicycles, three motorbikes, boxes of broken appliances, tools and general clutter from the house. I was shocked to hear that just weeks before, there were also nine lawnmowers waiting to be repaired. There was little space to move and the possibility of doing any work in these places was non-existent.

When I asked the man of the house why he was holding on to all these things, he was sincere in his belief that he would eventually fix and sell each of them. The overwhelming fact was that there was so much clutter, he didn't know where to begin, so he did nothing.

Used properly, garages and sheds provide work space for tools and storage, paints, gardening products and awkward household maintenance items that are too big, dangerous or messy to fit into your house. Most importantly, a garage is intended to store one of your most valuable assets – your car.

Take a look inside your garage or shed and see what is kept inside. How many of the items have you used in the last year? Has household clutter taken over the work space? Is it a dangerous, scary place with improper storage and ventilation? Could you begin a project without having to move things around?

Unfinished projects

Garages and work spaces often become littered with unfinished projects, such as household appliances that once cost a lot of money and now no longer work. Although in most cases you have purchased replacements, it seems like a waste of money to throw the broken items away, so they sit in your outbuildings for years, untouched and taking up space.

For a quick de-junking fix, get rid of all broken appliances that have been in the garage for more than one month. See also the suggestions on pages 131–2 for the best ways of recycling these items. You will probably find that this exercise clears a good deal of the accumulated clutter.

Before replacing a broken household appliance, make the commitment to have it fixed. By going without a replacement there is more motivation to get the job done. If it costs too much to fix, dispose of it immediately.

Tools

Over the centuries, tools have symbolized the rite of passage into manhood. They represent male energy and have been used by men over the ages to protect and provide for the family unit. They have also been a way for fathers to socialize with their male children and pass on family knowledge from generation to generation. In reality, many tools never get used, but the memories they evoke can make them difficult to dispose of.

Like most items housed in outbuildings, tools are often expensive purchases. This is another familiar reason for being unable to let go of items that are never used. Tools require maintenance to keep them in good condition and must be stored properly to avoid serious injuries.

If your garage or shed has become a dangerous, scary place filled with outdated tools and machinery, getting to grips with what you use and what is junk is essential.

Take a day to sort through your tools and make sure they are in good working order. Place like with like and immediately lose any duplicates you may have acquired over the years. Keep sharp and dangerous objects protected and stored in a safe location.

Paints and chemicals

Pots, cans and bottles containing paints and chemicals can be dangerous if not stored properly. It is essential to read the warning labels and make certain that all lids are tightly in place. Many substances must not be exposed to direct sunlight or high temperatures, so put them in appropriate places. Check the labels for use-by dates and safely dispose of any products that have expired.

Retaining paint that has been used for household projects can come in handy for touch-ups. Unfortunately, most of it dries out long before it is ever used again. A quick way of reducing the clutter is to gather all the paint pots and write a list of the make, colour and finish of each one. Also note which room the paint was used in. Immediately dispose of any paint that has dried up and any colours that are no longer relevant to your house. Pour small quantities of the colours you do want to retain into clean screwtop jars and label the outside with the room in which the paint was used. Get rid of the large cans and regain valuable space.

Sports equipment and exercise machines

Take an honest look at all the sports and exercise equipment you have collected in your garage and try to remember the last time they were used. If you can't recall, it's time to get ruthless and take back your space for the things you currently enjoy.

Old bicycles, lawnmowers and exercise machines that you haven't used in a year are prime candidates for recycling. These can be advertised in local newspapers for a small fee, and you'll even make back some of your initial investment.

Improvements

- Try to keep as much stuff as possible off the garage or shed floor. Many items are damaged by inclement weather, or by oil and grease leaking from old machinery.
- Utilize wall space and hang up items that occupy too much floor space. There are many clever storage racks that can be fixed to the wall to hold bicycles and sports equipment, keeping the floor space free to work and store cars.
- Sturdy metal shelving units are cheap to buy and provide good storage that can be accessed quickly. Keeping things neatly labelled makes them easier to find, so projects have a better chance of being completed.
- Tool boxes have little compartments designed to hold all the things that often get lost in bigger containers. Divide and conquer all your nails, bolts, screws and hooks into one compartmentalized box that you can find easily. It will save time when you're doing chores around the house.
- Keep all work surfaces clear of junk. Many large tools, such as electric drills, can be dangerous to use and require adequate space to maintain safety procedures. Getting rid of the junk can prevent serious accidents.

Kitchens

The great thing about kitchen clutter is that it doesn't usually hold any emotional attachments. What it does show is a lifestyle that has got out of control due to laziness or bad time management. The kitchen is the hub of the house and is the main place for social gatherings.

It is often the first room visited when people get home, so it can become a dumping ground for post, newspapers and shopping. It is also a magnet for internal junk from around the house that doesn't get put away.

Good cleaning routines are essential to prevent food clutter that is both unpleasant and dangerous and a hazard to health. Out-of-date foods can cause stomach upsets and unhygienic methods of storage can attract pests.

When you stop paying attention to the daily routines needed to safeguard your health and well-being, it is often a sign of problems in other areas of your life. Assessing the situation and taking the necessary steps to clean up your act will make you feel in control again.

We all have 'ghosts' in our kitchen – long-forgotten trendy appliances, such as yoghurt-makers, fondue pots and bread-making machines often take up space and never get used. These can make good car boot sale items, but there are certain legal requirements for selling electrical goods. See the advice on pages 127–8.

The kitchen should be used for food preparation and family or social gatherings. Does your kitchen allow you to make the most use of the space for these purposes?

Paperwork

Paper is the biggest contributor to cluttered work surfaces, making food preparation more of a chore than it needs to be.

There are, however, some good reasons for keeping papers in the kitchen. As the gathering point for the household, the kitchen makes a good 'communications centre', and is the best place to keep a calendar of events and important phone numbers. It often also serves as a gallery for children's schoolwork, but this must remain current and contained.

Any other papers should be food-related, such as take-away menus, and should be kept neatly in a confined space. Be sure to update them often to get rid of duplicates or outdated items.

Cupboards

Anything that has a door on it has the potential to become a scary place. Out of sight is out of mind, as the saying goes, and kitchen cupboards are classic places for things to get forgotten.

The best way to approach the problem of hidden kitchen clutter is to have a massive tidy-up and organize your things so that they save you time in doing your kitchen chores.

Begin by looking at where you store each type of kitchen item – pots and pans, glasses, dishes, tinned food and all other essentials. Make sure they are located near the area in which they are used. Ideally, your pots and pans should be near the cooker and your drinking glasses should be near the fridge. Planning how to use your kitchen will make your time in it feel like less of a chore.

When you remove everything from each cupboard, decide whether to use it or lose it. Check all use-by dates on food products and bin anything out of date. Go through all your drinking glasses and crockery and discard items with chips or cracks as these can cut you or harbour bacteria. Give the things you keep a thorough cleaning.

Sort all of your food by category and take an inventory of what you have. Keep related items together – baking products in one area, tinned foods in another – so you can quickly find what you need or know what to buy. It can save time and money by knowing what you own.

Appliances

Keep only the appliances used most frequently on top of the work surface. Those used less frequently should be placed in a more out-of-the-way location. Do not use your appliances as a means of storage. Keep pots and pans out of the oven and off the stove.

Recycling/Rubbish

Make sure to have enough containers to hold the amount of recycling or rubbish that your family generates each week. Have a designated location for them in the kitchen and make it a daily chore to look after them.

Cleaning routines

You may find it easier to keep an eye on kitchen clutter by establishing daily, weekly and monthly cleaning routines for your kitchen.

On a *daily* basis, you should wash your dishes (and empty the dishwasher, if you have one), and wipe down all the work surfaces.

On a *weekly* basis, you should clear out any food that has passed its use-by date and wipe down the inside of your refrigerator. You should also empty your rubbish bin and clean the floor.

On a *monthly* basis, you should tackle more difficult jobs such as cleaning the oven, and cleaning out drawers.

Improvements

- If you have limited space, don't keep huge reserves of bulky items such as detergents.
- Keeping your work surfaces free from clutter will motivate you to cook.
- Look at whether your current kitchen layout reflects how you use your kitchen, and, if possible, work towards having the ideal kitchen for your needs.

Lofts

The loft is the scariest hiding place in the house. I think of it as a graveyard – a final resting-place for things you never think about and many old issues that you have left unresolved. There is no time like the present to take action and lose all the clutter that is hidden away.

Anyone who has ever done a loft conversion will tell you that the space it provides is a wonderful asset. Not only do you get an additional living area and improvement in your quality of life, but the value of your house increases.

Unconverted loft space is fine to use for storage as long as you are able to discriminate between useful items and junk. You must be ruthless in your use it or lose it criteria.

One of the most important reasons to brave this scary area is safety. When we bury things away and don't want to deal with them, it is common to avoid visiting the place where they are stored. Unfortunately, many of the things thrown into the loft can deteriorate. Books and clothes can simply rot, while chemicals that are exposed to prolonged heat can pose a fire risk. Mountains of junk can also hide building defects that should really be addressed. Taking action for these reasons alone can avoid disaster in the future.

We often forget that items of value may be hidden away in the loft. Like our sentimental hoarder (see pages 108–9), who kept seven years' worth of unopened boxes in her garage, you don't know what's inside until you open them. You might be surprised to find some treasures. You might also find items that have lost value because of neglect. Dealing with the scary clutter can be worth money.

Assess whether your loft space allows you to access your items when needed. Can you easily identify the things you need to find? Are things safely stacked to avoid injuries? Is there enough space to get around? Is there any evidence of physical deterioration that could cause your possessions to get damaged by water or pests?

'Dead' appliances and broken objects
When I described the loft as a graveyard, I was thinking of all 'dead' items, such as old stereos, televisions and once-useful gadgets that would work if only they were fixed.

Often the only motivation for keeping these items is that they cost a lot when they were new. While it might be difficult to acknowledge that expensive objects are now kaput, appreciate the value they once brought you and use the recycling guide on pages 131–3 to help decide the best method of disposal.

Learn to deal with situations when they occur. If something breaks, fix it straight away. If it can't be repaired, dispose of it immediately, even if it is an object of sentimental value. Holding on to the remains makes you continue to suffer the loss. Let it go and move on.

Cardboard boxes

Some guarantees require you to retain an item's original packaging in the event that you need to send it back for repairs. If this is the case, flatten the box so that it consumes less space in the loft. If you have several flattened boxes, tie them with string to keep them tidy. If the guarantee has expired, or the appliance is broken, throw the packaging away.

Other clutter

Boxes often contain inner packaging made of polystyrene or bubble wrap. To cut down on the space it takes up, save only the most versatile pieces and bin the rest. Most of the other items that collect in your loft space are dealt with at the beginning of this chapter. Use the appropriate exercises to help you keep only the items that you truly value.

Improvements
- The loft is an ideal place to store items that are used occasionally rather than regularly, such as out-of-season clothing, garden furniture and Christmas decorations. Make sure you have easy access to the loft (a proper loft ladder is a good investment) so that it's not such a chore to put things up there or retrieve them.
- Set up a system to keep similar things together – books in one section, seasonal stuff in another. It will get you into the discipline of knowing what you have stored away.
- As cardboard boxes deteriorate over time, try to use sturdier options, such as plastic, for storing breakables. Protect individual items with bubble wrap or old newspapers.
- Many people store out-of-season clothing on garment rails, but it is important to keep them out of the sun to avoid fading. Dust can age fabrics even more quickly, so cover all clothing with breathable material, such as old sheets.
- Hang cedar or lavender in the loft to keep moths away.

Understairs

This is a doubly scary space for two reasons – its irregular size and its location. It is often difficult to install shelving under stairs because of height restrictions, so it is difficult to use all the space efficiently. Rather than accept the constraints of the space, some people become determined to use every nook and cranny, and jam loose items into the gaps. Clothes, carpets, soft furnishings, papers and other items that can be squeezed into irregularly shaped spaces find a welcome home in this scary place.

If your understairs cupboard is on a main thoroughfare in your house, it tends to become a dumping ground for whatever you bring indoors. Junk mail, plastic bags and paperwork are common invaders.

The other interesting fact about this space is that it seems to become invisible. The junk doesn't get noticed even when the stairs are not enclosed. Is there a magnetic force in this scary location?

Bad energy gets trapped in exposed corners, and the more you cram into them, the more negative energy you create. If your stairway is exposed, don't use it for storing bits and pieces. Leave it open or create a special use for the area that lets the energy circulate.

Take a look at what gathers under your stairs. An open-plan space should be more of a design statement than a storage solution. An enclosed cupboard under your stairs should be used for a specific purpose, namely storing items that are used nearby.

The understairs area was problematic for a contributor who had difficulty parting with sentimental items. The staircase was located in her lounge, which also doubled as her bedroom, and boxes of things she planned to deal with were simply stuck underneath. Thus, every night she faced boxes full of memories but took no action to release them.

We converted the understairs area into storage space for all her forms of entertainment. The television was mounted on an extended arm so that it could be folded away. The stereo, CDs, videos and other items were also moved into this underutilized space. I have always preferred to store bulky things like vacuum cleaners, brooms and suitcases under the stairs. The more you can limit the use of this area, the more efficiently you will be able to find the items you need, when you need them.

Unfinished projects

I often find that people use open understairs areas as temporary storage places for projects they intend to complete. As the items can be seen, they think they will remember to take action and move them on. Unfortunately, we tend to tune out reminders of things we haven't finished. See if some of the following situations apply to you:

- You have a stack of things to take to the charity shop. You bring them from where they were gathered and leave them under the stairs. They soon become part of the furnishings.
- You gather papers and other items for recycling in an area under the stairs. They don't get brought out on a regular basis, so they start to stack up.
- You begin to sort through a box of paperwork. It takes longer than you thought, and so you put it under the stairs to finish later. The paperwork gets forgotten and starts to pile up.

Routine dumping

Under the stairs is one of those places where we tend to put stuff at the end of the day. Because it has the appearance of being tucked away, it seems OK to let things collect. I have seen this area become a repository for junk mail, newspapers and office work. It is also a collecting point for outerwear when we come into the house. This is simply a bad routine that can be broken by developing a new routine to deal with these items daily. Make sure your children don't follow in your footsteps. Lead by example.

Improvements

- Get the energy moving in the understairs area of your house. Take out all the items that have collected and sort them into use it or lose it piles.
- To stop open-plan staircases becoming dumping grounds, install a large chest of drawers that fits the space. This will look good and provide much useful storage.
- Attach an attractive coat rack to the wall and it will look smart and be useful. Provided you keep the coats limited to the number of hooks and don't let clutter accumulate underneath, it can be an interesting focal point under the stairs.

Utility rooms

The utility room is a scary place that can quickly get out of control. Apart from housing the washing-machine and tumble-dryer, it is also used to store awkward items, such as ironing boards, vacuum cleaners and stepladders.

To understand how you let laundry pile up and clutter your space, you must analyze how well you and other members of your family look after their clothing. By getting into the routine of hanging up your clothes each night, you are able to air it and launder it less often. This can save lots of money on dry-cleaning bills and lots of time doing the laundry. You will also extend the life of your garments, as over-laundering puts additional wear and tear on them.

Household cleaning products also take up lots of space in utility rooms. Recycling or binning old bottles and boxes of detergent as soon as they are empty can help to keep work surfaces clear and give you an area in which to fold your clothing.

The utility room should be used strictly as a space to launder your clothes, not to store them. Each bulky item should have an assigned space and be put back in the same place as a matter of routine. Throwing things into any available space wastes time and creates chaos.

Laundry

You probably learned your cleaning skills from watching your parents do the chores when you were younger. As you gain independence and no longer have to answer to anyone's rules but your own, you begin to set in place habits that can last a lifetime. What do your laundry habits say about you?

Follow these quick tips to stay on top of laundry clutter.
- Save time by sorting your laundry when you take it off. Invest in a laundry basket that has divisions for light and dark clothing.
- As you load the washing-machine, inspect each garment for spots/stains that need pre-treatment and address any minor repairs, such as loose buttons and undone hems. A sewing kit with all the basics is a laundry-room essential.
- Have everything to hand to deal with the finished washing. If you hang things up to dry, be sure you have enough hangers available where you need them.

- Make it a new habit to see things through to the end. Don't leave wet washing in the machine. If you do, your clothes will become musty and you may never be able to remove the smell. Similarly, remove items from the dryer as soon as they are done. You can cut your ironing by 50 per cent if you give the proper care and attention to your clothes when taking them from the dryer. Don't over-dry them: this makes ironing more difficult and adds wear and tear to the fabrics.
- Fold and put away every single item in its proper place as soon as you have finished the laundry. In a big household, try to put each person's clothes in a different coloured laundry basket to indicate their final destination. Things will stay pressed longer if you take the time and effort to put them away properly, and save re-ironing when you next want to wear something.

Improvements
- Using creative storage solutions in the utility room can make doing your laundry and other housekeeping chores a breeze. By not having to fight your way to the things you need, you will spend less time completing the process.
- Shelves over the door can increase your storage capacity significantly. Use wall racks racks to hold your iron and board, vacuum cleaner hoses, brooms and other tall items that tend to fall over. Cascading racks will hold shirts that have been ironed and prevent wrinkles.
- Store cleaning products in wall cabinets. Make sure to read any caution labels for special storage requirements.
- Under-sink storage, if part of the utility room, is a good place to keep small, unsightly items, such as buckets, dustpans and brushes.

Letting go of emotions

Are you willing to let it go? Your willingness and intention to let go of the cause of clutter will determine how successfully you are able to conquer your clutter forever. Living clutter-free must be a conscious choice and requires you to have discipline and never lose focus of what is going on around you. It means that you are constantly connected to the present moment.

Several of our contributors had clutter-busted areas of their homes in the past, to find that it returned to the same state within 12 months. On one occasion, a sister of one of the contributors even went to the trouble of renting a skip so that she could clear and redecorate her sister's guestroom when she was away on holiday. Although all the junk was thrown away, more junk took its place because the root of the problem was never addressed. Our contributor collected junk because shopping became a replacement activity after her retirement. If you don't look at the origin of your problem, it is more than likely that the situation will recur.

On many occasions, people try to force themselves to change, often as a result of external pressures from other people or the prevailing circumstances. Until you are truly receptive to the idea of change, you are not signalling your inner readiness to take action. This is the greatest problem in curing addictions. Anyone who has attempted to give up smoking or any other addictive behaviour or habit before having truly resolved to do so will understand that a cure is not possible in that situation.

Emotional release

Letting go of emotions can be painful, but sometimes it is simply fun. We had many laughs while going through some of the silly things that our contributors held on to for emotional reasons. We found clothing so old that it had come back into fashion, although the body that originally wore it had 'matured' out of it. Many horrid presents were uncovered and released with a laugh rather than guilt and shame. Laughing is great therapy because it helps you to shift energy blockages in your body. Allow yourself to see the funny side of the situation to achieve balance.

Looking through your possessions can also revive wonderful memories that remind us what it is like to be happy. Smiling is great beauty treatment because it stimulates the muscles in your face, but also makes you feel really good. It serves a purpose and brings you pleasure.

Moments of great drama were captured during our filming when, after selling or giving away the most useable items, we were able to crush the accumulated junk and debris of many years. Getting rid of the clutter in your life can be a profoundly moving experience, felt on the emotional, mental and physical levels of your being.

One of our most emotional programmes involved a contributor who had a terrible time letting go of her sentimental things. She had successfully discarded many physical reminders of bad experiences in her life relating to work and her failed marriage. In fact, the physical act of throwing these items in the crusher allowed a major blockage of energy in her home and life to be released.

However, the issues underlying her attachment to sentimental items were really quite complex. At the age of five she had experienced a traumatic event through ill health that made her feel abandoned. Since that time she had needed constant reassurance that she was loved, so she had retained all the letters and cards that had been sent to her over the years by family and friends.

This is not a problem that can be solved overnight. It is necessary to bring your awareness to who you are at the present moment and focus your attention on all reasons that you are loveable. This can be a very difficult task for those with low self-esteem.

Sometimes the process of letting go of past emotions can bring back memories of traumas that you may not have known were unresolved. It is often at this time that you are ready to learn the lessons from the situation and let it go. However, it may require professional help to get you through the process.

Exercises to expel negative emotions

Review the goal-setting exercise in Chapter 2 for any emotional goals that need attention (such as dealing with grief following bereavement, low self-esteem, or living in the past). Make a list, starting with the easiest goal, then look at the following exercises and choose the one that seems most suited to your situation.

Breathe and let go

1. Think about an inner problem that you feel ready to let go of, such as anger that you associate with a particular situation. If you feel you have many such problems, pick the easiest one for you to give up at this moment. Think about what colour you associate with the problem.
2. Take in a deep, slow and smooth breath to the count of one. As you do so, imagine breathing in the beautiful healing colours of white, gold and violet.
3. As you release this breath, blow out the colour representing the negative energy. Repeat this process seven times, controlling your breath and expelling the negative colour on each occasion.

This exercise really works. Because you are willing to release your problem, it is easy to visualize it leaving through your breath. Once you release this negative energy, it is gone for good, allowing the higher vibrational energies associated with the colours of gold, violet and white to take its place. This process raises your level of consciousness, making you feel lighter and giving you the energy to continue progressing down your new path.

Stress relief

Energy blockages are a common reason for holding on to things, so release the stress in your body and you will be freer to release your clutter.

This is a three-stage process that focuses on controlling your breathing, relaxing your body and calming your mind. By practising these three techniques, it is possible to become more aware of how you process stress and the physical effects it can have on your body.

Control your breathing

Most people never think about their breathing. From the time we are born, it is something we take for granted until perhaps a cold or asthma makes us appreciate what we usually ignore.

It took me many years to learn a new breathing pattern to enable me to swim properly, so it is important to persevere in re-educating your breathing techniques to break the stressful routines.

1. Stand in front of a mirror and take two deep breaths in and out. Do your shoulders and neck move? Do you have problems with tension in your neck or shoulders?

If you do breathe using your neck and shoulders, you will probably find that these areas collect tension. With every breath, you are putting stress into your body.

2. Focus your attention on your lungs. Take in two deep breaths, relaxing the shoulders downward. Feel the difference that breathing properly makes in your neck and shoulders. To become more aware of how you breathe, check your breathing each time you walk past a mirror.

Take in more oxygen

Breathing deeply helps to oxygenate the blood and the brain. It also helps to dispel carbon dioxide. You will have heard the advice 'Take a deep breath' when you need to calm yourself or prepare for a stressful situation. Doing it more often will benefit your mental clarity.

1. Breathe in as deeply as you can. Breathe in a bit more. Try again a third time and, if you are able, a fourth time.
2. Breathe out as deeply as you can. Breathe out a bit more. Try again, a third time, and a fourth if you are able.
3. Repeat these steps eight times.

Physical relaxation

By physically relaxing the body and acquiring awareness of each part of it, you will feel better and be able to release energy blockages. Many forms of yoga use relaxation techniques to strengthen both mind and body, so find out what local classes are on offer.

Aches and pains that are not associated with any illness may be caused by stress, and with time these can become chronic and even debilitating. However, it is possible to release them with the following relaxation exercises.

1. Sit in a comfortable chair, feet on the ground and the back well supported.
2. Focus your attention on your toes and feet. Think about how they feel. Now think about how they feel when walking through grass, on sand or in the sea. Become aware of your feet, and with each breath in, breathe love into your feet.
3. Now focus on your ankles. Become aware of every detail of them, and with each breath in, send your ankles love.
4. Continue this process, focusing your attention on each part of the body – shins, knees, hips, lower body, middle body and upper body, neck, back, shoulders, head and face.

Try doing this exercise before you get out of bed in the morning and when you first get into bed at night.

If you would like someone to guide you through the process, there are many excellent tapes and compact discs available.

Mental calming

There are many techniques for calming the mind. Meditation, for example, focuses the mind on a singular sound, word, colour, or shape. The aim is to learn a relaxation cue that will help clear the mind of unnecessary thoughts.

Meditation

1. Sit upright if you are in bed, or in a chair as described in the previous exercise.
2. Take in a deep, slow and smooth breath to the count of four, then release it. Continue until you feel your breathing is relaxed.
3. Focus your mind on one object, such as a pebble. Think only about this object. If you find other thoughts coming into your head, gently let them go by and come back to them when you have finished your mental calming.

Visualization of mental relaxation

Another method is to create a visualization as described in the following exercise.

1. Repeat steps 1–3 of the previous exercise to prepare yourself.
2. Imagine walking in the most beautiful fields filled with wild flowers and beautiful grasses. Look at all the colours. Smell the flowers. Take in every detail of the space. Breathe in the country air and feel the warmth of the sun on your body. Use any scene that you enjoy.

The on-going programme

Create a peaceful oasis in your mind that you can retreat to for relaxation whenever you feel the need. Practise the technique that feels most comfortable for twenty minutes in the morning and evening.

When you are able to let go of emotional debris, you will find it easier to let go of the physical manifestation of it. Your aches and pains may improve, and you may have more energy to help you clear the physical junk as well.

It is not healthy to hold on to stale habits, emotions and physical remainders of things that happened in the past. It prevents you from living in the present and promotes low self-esteem, which in turn can cause ill health on the physical level.

Don't let your emotions build up to unmanageable levels. Learn to take the necessary actions every day to release this negative energy pattern. Observe each situation objectively, dealing only with the present moment. This removes any old feelings, such as anger and guilt, and allows you to deal with the situation unemotionally.

It takes practice to live in the present moment, so don't give up. Thinking of the following words has helped me to achieve my goals. Perhaps they will help you too.

'The past is history. Tomorrow a mystery. Today is a gift, which is why it is called the present.' Anonymous

CASE STUDY: DOWNSIZING AFTER DIVORCE

The trauma associated with divorce is often made worse when it includes moving from a large home to a smaller one. Possessions must be divided, but you will still be left with things that have associations with a painful past.

A mother and her two children moved from their large, five-bedroom home to a two-bedroom coach house seven years ago following a stressful divorce. The mother gave her son and daughter the bedrooms and for two years she slept in the living room, eventually taking over a bedroom when her daughter went off to university and then travelling. Her daughter has now left the home to start her career and she is living at home with her 21-year-old son.

During the marriage, the family moved nine times in eleven years. Once the marriage was dissolved, the mother wanted a house that had enough character to be a long-term base for her family. She wanted to create a stable environment for her family after so many disruptions.

She had many lovely pieces of furniture from her family that were hidden away and never used. Her new home could not accommodate all of the stuff from the larger home and much of it ended up filling the garage space and was left unopened until the past year. Lots more ended up scattered throughout the house as a constant reminder of their current circumstances.

She held on to papers associated with her past traumas that had related to a period in hospital and an illness that left her with little to no energy for several years. She also suffered from low esteem based on early life traumas that caused her to retain all items that showed people cared about her.

By confronting her junk and letting go of past traumas, we tried to enable her to take action and deal in the present moment. The situation was improved; however, the revisit showed there were many areas that still needed to be dealt with.

5

Trash or treasure?

Discovering hidden treasures is one of the benefits of coming to grips with what you own. Learning to value and care for your possessions allows you to see the real beauty of the objects that you choose to live with.

In this chapter Mark Franks offers you the benefit of his extensive knowledge of the antiques and collectables market to help you realize the full value of your hidden treasures. As well as providing detailed information about how to date and clean your rediscovered treasures, he also suggests the most profitable ways in which to dispose of them. Whatever you do, don't rush off to an auction or car boot sale without reading his advice first. It could save you a lot of money and heartache.

As with all the exercises in this book, approach each task methodically and be prepared to dedicate several hours of uninterrupted time to complete it. You'll be glad you did.

Rediscovered treasures

So, you think you might have a valuable antique on your hands? This section advises you on what to look out for in items such as furniture, china and jewellery, and then how to clean your treasure without damaging its value.

Important
Before attempting to clean your pieces, remember the following:
- Not every object benefits from being cleaned.
  Read the specific advice given in each category below.
- Use only the substances and methods suggested.
  Using harsher treatment could ruin your treasure.
- Test a small, hidden area first.

Some of the big auction houses offer free valuations and advice.

Essential cleaning kit
- Washing-up liquid
- Old toothbrushes
- Cotton wool and cotton buds
- Kitchen paper
- Newspaper
- Milk
- Vinegar
- Bottlebrush
- Green garden stick
- Bleach
- Full-sugar cola
- Brown sauce
- Dry, empty washing-up bottle
- Cigarette ash
- *And most importantly*, lots of elbow grease!

Furniture

You've been through all your possessions, sifting out the rubbish, and you've found furniture that is old, dirty and of unknown origin. To establish whether it's worth anything, you have to find out how old it is, and there are various ways of doing that.

Dating furniture

The main problem with establishing the age of furniture is that popular designs have been produced by different people at different times, and it can be hard to tell the copies from the original. To further confuse the uninitiated, craftsmen developed techniques to make new pieces look old – this practice became an art form in itself.

Even when the style of a piece indicates a particular period, dates still tend to be approximate because cities, especially London, led the way in furniture-making, and rural areas sometimes lagged up to 20 years behind.

The most reliable way of dating furniture is to examine how it is made.

Construction

Every piece of furniture reveals its age when you look at it closely. Generally speaking, the simpler the construction, the older the piece, but that's not to say it was put together crudely. Many of the construction techniques remained the same for centuries, but as tools improved, so did the delicacy of the work.

The following characteristics of furniture-making will help you to make a preliminary assessment of the age of your 'treasure'.

Seventeenth century
- Pegged joints (pegs of wood hammered into holes that run through the two pieces of wood that form a joint). If the pegs are original, they stand slightly proud of the piece.
- Drawers made of thick timber.
- Dovetails (usually three per joint) very coarse and big.
- Grooves cut into the sides of drawers which slot over runners for smooth operation. (Drawers from later periods simply slide in and out on their base.)
- Crude nails, known as 'five clout', used to attach the sides of drawers.
- Oak commonly used, and walnut introduced in 1675.

Early eighteenth century
- Oak in decline and mahogany introduced to replace walnut. (Rural craftsmen continued to use oak, ash, elm and beech.)
- Veneers hand-cut and as thick as a 20 pence piece. (Saw marks can be seen on the underside of the veneer if it has lifted away from the piece.)
- 'Pear drop' handles with a circular back plate.
- Wooden knobs made of rosewood or mahogany, with handmade metal thread and 'nut' to attach them.
- Escutcheons (protective plates around keyholes) made of brass (or can be mother of pearl in other types of wood).

Post-1740
- 'Batwing' handles, with brass back plate shaped like a bat in flight and a U-shaped handle. Also made with a pierced back plate.
- 'Swan neck' handles introduced – a wide U-shape attached at either end to a round disc.
- Dovetails finer and as many as six to a joint.
- Leather casters, supported on a brass rod, introduced in 1755.
- Cockbeading, a decorative rounded edge often made of mahogany and applied to veneered pine drawers, introduced in 1770s.
- Brass casters introduced in 1785.
- Grain of wood runs from front to back in base of drawers.
- Drawer linings made of oak.
- Plain bracket feet used from 1720 to 1780, more decorative ogee bracket feet until 1785, then splayed bracket feet until 1810.

Nineteenth century
- Drawer bases made of pine in cheaper quality pieces.
- Blue lining paper sometimes glued to bottom of drawers.
- Turned wooden knobs introduced, with wooden thread and 'nut' to attach them.
- Batwing handles made of tin, then anodized to resemble dull copper or brass.
- Brass escutcheons had rounded bottoms from 1850, and squarer bottoms from 1870.
- Veneers machine-cut and as thin as a business card.
- Lathe-turned round feet used from 1837.
- Machine-made dovetails, recognizable by being identical, square and perfectly spaced, introduced from 1880.

Key dates

1714–60: Early Georgian
Furniture of this period was very square in design.

1760–1811: Late Georgian
More graceful curves and intricate carving were introduced during this period.

1812–30: Regency
A transitional period from the squareness of Georgian style to the rounded shapes of the Victorian era. Regency furniture often had turned feet and rounded columns.

1830–37: William IV
A slightly more extreme, flamboyant version of Regency style.

1837–1901: Victorian
Furniture, especially feet and handles and the inner frames of chairs, became very rounded during this period. Popular woods included walnut, mahogany and rosewood.

1870–1900: Arts & Crafts Movement
A return to unfussy pieces, strong in Celtic motifs, inlay piercing and leaded glass. Most of this furniture is heavy and angular. William Morris is the most well known proponent of this style.

1880–1914: Art Nouveau
A style distinguished by decorative, flowing lines and flower motifs.

1901–10: Edwardian
Machine-made furniture became commonplace and pieces became square again.

1920s–1930s: Art Deco
A glitzy movement characterized by simple, geometric shapes and the abundant use of chrome and black. Charles Rennie Mackintosh was a key influence in this style.

What type of wood?

Furniture can be made from virtually any kind of wood – there are hundreds, if not thousands, of different types. Listed below are the ones you'll most commonly encounter in households. Pull out a drawer and look at the carcass: this will show you the true colour and grain of the wood.

Mahogany is a deep red colour, unless it's been in the sun for years, when it becomes a light terracotta or oak colour. The grain is tightly packed, so you won't be able to dig a fingernail into it. It has very few knots.

Oak is a hardwood that comes in various shades of brown and has a very tight grain. Like mahogany, oak has few knots.

Pine is yellowish and becomes greyer with time. It has lots of knots and is soft enough to dig your fingernail into it.

Plywood consists of many thin sheets of timber glued together and was used to make cheaper furniture from the late 1920s.

How to clean wood

As wood ages, it acquires a sheen and depth of colour called 'patina', which is a very desirable characteristic. In order to preserve this, it is essential to clean lightly, removing only dirt.

If the item is veneered, i.e. has a thin layer of fine wood over a cheaper carcass, make sure no water gets underneath the veneer, or it will make it lift. If the veneer is already damaged, take care not to catch your cloth on it and make the problem worse.

- Fill a bowl with warm water and add a tiny amount of washing-up liquid. Dip a clean cloth in the water and wring it out well.
- Rub the wood with the damp cloth, then dry it with a fresh cloth immediately.
- Very dirty pieces can be cleaned with a solution of 2 parts methylated spirits, 2 parts pure turpentine (not turps substitute) and 2 parts vinegar. Shake well, as the mixture tends to separate, and then apply to a small, hidden test area (not bare wood) with cotton wool or a clean cloth.
- Rub very gently and you should see the dirt lifting, leaving the patina behind.
- This is a strong solution, so work delicately on a small area at a time and wipe it immediately with a clean cloth.
- Cleaned items need a good polish to bring out the beauty of the wood. Avoid those containing silicon (which builds up layer by layer and makes the wood a milky colour) and linseed oil (which both

darkens the wood over time and attracts dirt) and find one that contains beeswax, carnauba wax and a solvent such as turpentine, white spirit or paraffin.

Heat marks and scratches

The ghostly white marks left by hot cups and dishes on polished wood are horrible disfigurements, but they can be safely and easily removed with burnishing cream, available from most DIY stores. Tackle a small area at a time, checking your progress as you go.

An alternative method is to use cotton wool dampened with spit and dipped into cigarette ash. Rub gently into the affected area, then dry straight away.

Light scratches can be removed by rubbing in scratch-covering liquid, also available from DIY stores. Deeper scratches may require professional help.

Cleaning and reviving leather

Quite often, a quick rub with a damp cloth followed by wiping with a dry one will be all that is needed. White spirit, applied sparingly, may also work the trick.

Leather that requires more reviving than these methods provide will benefit from a preparation that you can have made up in larger chemists' shops.

British Museum leather polish

- 30 g hexane
- 200 ml anhydrous lanolin
- 30 ml cedarwood oil
- 14 g beeswax

Apply this mixture with a clean cloth and allow to dry overnight. Wipe off with a clean cloth.

If the leather is thoroughly dry, apply natural beeswax and let it soak in overnight. Polish with a clean shoe brush, using the appropriate colour shoe polish if the leather requires it.

Never use saddle soap as it reacts with the leather and, over time, will do a lot of damage.

China

How can you tell if anything in your box of china oddments is noteworthy or valuable? The first thing to do is look on the bottom of each object and see if there are any marks. All the major manufacturers have their own symbols that they stamp on their wares, and you can find books about them in your local library.

Makers' marks
Look out for the following notable names:

Belleek	Minton
Beswick	Poole
Bow	Shelly
Carlton Ware	Spode
Chelsea	Susie Cooper
Claris Cliff	Sylvac
Denby	Wade
Derby	Wedgwood
Doulton	Worcester
Mason	

Registration marks

The next thing to do is find the date of the piece. This can often be done by looking up the registration mark. On some pieces dating from 1842 to 1883, the mark is a diamond containing the letter 'R' with a 'D' next to it. Other letters at each corner of the diamond tell you the day, month and year of manufacture.

From 1884 the diamond was replaced by a registration number. Again, you can easily decode the number by checking in a good reference book.

Other china-dating tips

- Printed marks appear on china made after 1800.
- The name of the pattern and the royal arms sometimes appear on china after 1810.
- The words 'Bone China' were not widely used before 1844.
- The word 'Royal' was first used from 1850.
- The word 'Limited' or 'Ltd' first appeared in 1861.
- The words 'Trade Mark' may appear on china made after 1862.
- The word 'England' appears from 1880.

- 'Made in England' appears from 1910 onwards.
- Poole china adopted the word 'Limited' from 1925.
- Sylvac used a daisy-style mark until 1935, then changed to SylvaC with a capital 'C' at the end.
- The letter 'R' inside a circle indicates manufacture after 1955.
- Shelly used the word 'Ltd' from 1966.

How to clean china
- Always clean one item at a time, and never use a dishwasher.
- Half-fill a washing-up bowl with warm, not hot, water, line the base with some old hand towels and add a little washing-up liquid.
- Immerse your object in the water, but avoid holding it by the handle as this is the weakest part. (If the handle comes off, the value drops dramatically.)
- Use an old toothbrush and cotton buds to clean the object thoroughly, but don't be too vigorous or you might damage it.
- A weak solution of bleach can be used to hide hairline cracks on plain white china, but don't let it come into contact with patterns or gilding.
- Rinse the object in clean water and leave to stand.

These cleaning instructions apply to china only. Some pottery like terracotta and earthenware should not be dipped in water – as it is porous, it will stain.

Glass

Glass dates back thousands of years, but the glass industry worldwide really came of age in the eighteenth century. Antique glass from this period should be clear and have a greyish black hue. Look for small scratches on the underside of the foot – these marks should be visible on pieces that have been used over the centuries. Where the stem of the glass joins the bowl, look to see whether it is a perfect joint – if not, it is an applied stem which means the glass was made in separate pieces and then joined together. Pressed glass, produced in Britain from 1841, has a distinguishing seam where the pieces were joined.

New or old?

If you have a decanter and are not sure if the stopper is original, there is a simple test to establish the truth. Insert the stopper, give it a half turn to the left, then hold the decanter by the stopper just above a bed or sofa. If the stopper is original, the decanter will not fall. If it does fall, at least it won't break. Always release the stopper afterwards.

If the stopper of your decanter is stuck, pour some olive oil around it and leave in a warm place, such as an airing cupboard, overnight. The stopper will slip out easily.

How to clean glass

- Follow the same procedure as for china (see page 119), but always dry the object thoroughly to avoid streaks.
- To remove stains from a decanter, wash the item, then half-fill it with vinegar, or water to which household soda crystals or a denture-cleaning tablet has been added. Leave it to stand overnight, minus the stopper. (Take care that none of these liquids come into contact with any gilding on the exterior.)
- Get a thin stick, such as a plant support, wrap kitchen paper round one end of it and wipe inside the decanter.
- Empty out the liquid, then wipe inside again with clean kitchen paper.
- If the stains persist, you can repeat the procedure. A more expensive option is to get the decanter cleaned professionally.

Other materials and objects

Mirrors

How to clean mirrors

- If the mirror is very dirty, begin by wiping the glass with methylated spirit.
- Half-fill a washing-up bowl with warm water and stir in 2 dessertspoons of vinegar, mixing well.
- Immerse a clean, soft cloth in the solution, then wring it out and wipe over the mirror. (Keep the frame as dry as possible.)
- Use a dampened cotton bud to get into the corners.
- Screw up a sheet of old newspaper and use it to dry the mirror.

Paintings

The world of art is vast and impossible to cover here in any detail. If you suspect you have something of value, consult a local dealer or one of the large auction houses that offers a free identification and valuation service.

How to clean paintings

- **Never** attempt to clean paintings yourself. This is a specialist task, so always seek out expert advice.
- If you want to clean a non-valuable oil painting (with a shiny finish) clean with a cotton bud lightly dampened in your mouth, then gently roll it over the surface of the painting in a small test area in the corner. Do not rub or scrub. This method is known as 'spit cleaning'.

Marble

How to clean marble

- The traditional way of cleaning marble is to dip half a lemon into rock salt and to rub it over the surface. Wipe clean with a damp cloth.
- I prefer to use a damp cloth with a little detergent and a lot of elbow grease.

Ivory

How to clean ivory

Ivory yellows with age, but don't be tempted to try any bleaching process, such as soaking it in warm milk. The liquid will simply make the ivory swell and split, and encourage mould to grow.

- Use a cotton bud dampened in your mouth to rub off any dirt, then buff with a clean, soft cloth.

Tortoiseshell

Trinket boxes and combs were often made of tortoiseshell.

How to clean tortoiseshell

- Rub a little olive oil into the surface to feed it and restore the shine, then polish with a clean cloth.

Hairbrushes and combs

Attractive dressing-table sets are popular items with collectors.

How to clean hairbrushes and combs

- Remove any hairs from the items, then soak in sterilizing fluid designed for babies' bottles. Make sure the back of the brush doesn't get wet.

Bakelite and plastic

How to clean Bakelite and plastic

- Use car colour-restoring fluid or a brass cleaner, and polish with a soft cloth.
- You can also use brass-cleaning impregnated wadding.

Gold

How to clean gold

- If cleaning jewellery, check that any stones in it are secure before starting.
- The gentlest method of cleaning stones is to rub them with a cotton bud dampened in your mouth. Alternatively, soap and water may be used, but never put aquamarine in hot water.
- Use crumpled newspaper to polish gold rings – the result is amazing.
- Very dirty objects may be immersed in a glass of non-diet cola and left overnight. This does not damage the stones.

Silver

Real silver, having a purity of at least 92.5 per cent, carries an assay mark, which shows a lion walking towards the left. It will also have the mark of the particular assay office where it was tested.

Well-known assay marks

London – leopard's head
Birmingham – anchor
Edinburgh – castle
Dublin – harp with crown above
Chester – shield containing three wheat sheaves
Exeter – three-towered castle
Sheffield – crown

The year of assay is indicated by a letter, which was changed in alphabetical order year by year. When the end of the alphabet was reached, the font of the lettering or the shape of the box was changed.

Every piece of silver will also carry a maker's mark. Early ones tended to be pictorial, but since the early eighteenth century, initials have been used. Lists of these can be found in any good reference book on silver.

How to clean silver

- Small silver objects may be cleaned by immersing them in brown sauce or rubbing them with cigarette ash.
- To clean a large silver object, line a washing-up bowl with aluminium foil, fill with boiling water and add 2 dessertspoons of soda crystals.
- Immerse the tarnished item for one or two minutes, then remove it using wooden tongs. Never use rubber gloves, as these will mark the silver.
- Rinse the item in clean water and dry with kitchen paper.

Silver-plate

There are two common types of silver plate. The first of these, invented in Sheffield in the 1760s, is copper to which a thin layer of silver has been applied. Electro-plated nickel silver (EPNS), invented in the 1840s, is nickel plated with silver.

Both Sheffield plate and EPNS are worth a lot less than solid silver, but there are some very collectable items around.

How to clean silver-plate

- Follow the instructions for cleaning solid silver.

Bronze

Under no circumstances attempt to clean bronze! Over the years, the colour of bronze changes gradually and the rich-coloured patina is what makes bronze items so desirable to collectors.

- If you have a build-up of dust, simply blow it or dust gently with a feather duster. Do not wipe it with a cloth.

Brass and copper

Many people like buying discoloured brass and copper for the simple pleasure of cleaning it and discovering what really lies underneath the tarnish. In fact, it looks just the same underneath, but more shiny! If you don't plan to keep the objects yourself, leave the cleaning to the eventual buyer.

How to clean brass and copper

- **Don't** attempt to clean it, no matter how tempted you may be. Let the buyer clean it.

Aluminium

How to clean aluminium

- Colour-restoring fluid, commonly used on cars, will restore the sheen.

Tinplate

How to clean tinplate

- Use wadding impregnated with brass polish, but apply very carefully, and stop immediately if any paint starts to come off.

Clocks, watches and cameras

How to clean clocks, watches & cameras

- **Never** use spray lubricants or any type of oil on the mechanisms.
- An empty and completely dry washing-up bottle may be used to puff air into the works and blow out any dust.

Dealing with clocks, watches and cameras is specialist work, so my advice is to leave cleaning to the buyer or an expert.

Don't ever attempt to take apart a clock – you will not be able to reassemble it correctly, and it's not worth the risk.

Garden furniture and ornaments

How to clean garden furniture and ornaments

- Many people like outdoor items to look weathered, so restrict yourself to brushing off dirt and cobwebs.
- Benches, statues and plant pots with a weathered look are more popular with collectors than pristine items! Smear some natural yoghurt on a new plant pot, leave it outside for a season, and the resulting mould growth will make it look fifty years old.
- Hardwood furniture can be treated with special preservative oil available from DIY shops.

Are you ready to sell?

Right, you've sorted out your stuff, cleaned it up, checked out the marks and decided how much things are worth. The next step is to find a good place to sell them.

Selling from home

Rather than spend time and money carting your possessions somewhere else, why not start at your own home? Invite your friends round for an impromptu sale and you'll be surprised at how much fun everyone has and how much money you make.

If you have trouble valuing certain items because they're not in any reference books, let your friends help. You don't have to accept their suggestions, but they might provide useful guidelines.

Garage sales

If you want to attract a larger number of people than the impromptu sale above, why not print some flyers giving details of the sale, and distribute them in your neighbourhood? You could also place an advertisement in your local newspaper. Make sure your chosen date doesn't clash with any other fêtes or fairs.

Price up all the items beforehand and recruit some people to help you on the day of the sale. Anything you don't want to sell should be removed from the garage.

Accept cash only, never cheques, and keep the money with you in a bumbag for security.

Car boot sales

Local newspapers or freesheets often list forthcoming events, so look at these sources first and choose two or three venues to visit. These first trips to car boot sales are purely for research purposes – you won't be selling anything just yet.

Be prepared for an early start. In my experience, the best sales get going at 6 a.m. on Sunday morning. When you arrive, note the number of stalls: if there are less than a dozen, move on to the next sale. Look at the buyers: are they dealers or people like you?

Get chatting to a seller and ask if they attend this sale regularly. If so, do they think it is a good place to sell? Can they recommend any other good sales?

Weigh up the information you've gathered and decide which sale you're going to attend as a seller. Find out the entrance fee and what time you need to get there. (Some sales allocate places on a first come, first served basis, so you might need to be early, especially in summer.)

What do you need to take?

Table for displaying your wares. Most people use a wallpaper table with folding legs because it's easy to fit into the car. A plastic garden table with detachable legs is also suitable. Whichever you choose, make sure it's solid and sturdy. I've seen lots of people arrive with tables that turn out to be wonky or broken, so they can't use them.

Folding chair because you'll definitely want to sit down at some point.

Newspapers and carrier bags for wrapping china and glass. You might also find it useful to take a pack of plasters as china and glass can cause injuries.

Plastic sheet – available from DIY stores, is useful for covering up your stuff if it starts to rain.

Umbrella – essential whatever the weather: it can keep you dry or provide shade.

Spare shoes and warm coat – very useful during cold weather, but don't forget to take suntan lotion for the hot spells.

Bumbag – the best way to keep money safe. You'll need a few notes and some coins for change, but remember how much you start out with so you'll be able to calculate your profit. Take your entrance fee separately so you don't start dipping into your float. Accept cash only, and never take a cheque under any circumstances.

Food and drink – not all sales have refreshment stalls, and the presence of a stall one week doesn't mean it will be there the next.

Toilet roll – you'll really thank me for this suggestion, as the facilities at most car boot sales are rarely good.

What can you sell?

It is against the law to sell alcohol or any form of tobacco, so don't be tempted to take your unwanted cigarettes if you have just given up.

It is also illegal to sell counterfeit goods, such as pirate videos, CDs and clothing.

Electrical goods must be tested to ensure they comply with safety regulations (available from your local council offices). You are responsible if someone is hurt by an electrical appliance you have sold. If you are uncertain about the wiring, cut off the flex close to the appliance so that the purchaser will have to rewire the article before using it.

Pricing and packing your wares

Buy some small sticky labels and put the price on each item before you leave home. Get a friend to help you if you're not sure what to charge. People like to haggle at sales, so have a reserve price in mind and don't let dealers, or anyone else, intimidate you into accepting less.

Wrap breakables in newspaper and put them in cardboard boxes. Old blankets are useful for wedging between the boxes to stop them sliding around.

Put the table in last because it has to come out first.

Setting up

Arrive at the sale with plenty of time to spare and try to find a space free of puddles. Sell from the side of your car rather than the back – this gives you more room so that you can see all your items laid out. If you have lots of valuable items, don't put them all out at once, but keep your car locked at all times and don't leave any valuables on show.

When you set up the table make sure that any valuable items are nearest you and everything you have on sale is visible.

Car boot sale regulars tend not to set up their stalls straight away. The more professional ones look around for a complete novice like you and buy some of your more desirable items to sell on at higher prices.

Other sellers might try to cadge boxes and packing from you. Don't be a soft touch: you might need them later yourself.

If you get very busy, let the customers wrap up their own purchases. It's an informal situation and most people are happy to do so.

How to spot dealers

Ordinary punters tend to wander about aimlessly at sales, stopping to look at anything that catches their eye. Dealers are exactly the opposite. They tend to arrive early and move quickly from stall to stall creaming off the best buys. This is their job, not a hobby, so they are interested only in making money.

Dealers have lots of tricks up their sleeves, so be prepared. Let's say they pick up an £8 teapot, knock it down to £6 and you accept. They hold on to the teapot without paying for it, then pick up another item, such as a £9 vase, offer you £7 and you accept. Now they add the two prices together, a total of £13, and offer you £10 for the pair. It's cheeky but it works, and you can lose a lot of money if several items are involved.

Antique shops

Perhaps you have some items that are just too good for a car boot sale, or maybe they are too large to fit into your car. This is where antique dealers come in. Take the actual item or a photograph of it along to the antique shop and ask for an opinion. You're not forced to sell if you're not happy with what they say.

Antique dealers are expert at not revealing what they truly think of a piece, but if you get even a glimmer of interest, play it cool. Ask them to make you an offer, and don't reveal the minimum figure that you will accept. It pays to get more than one opinion, so move on to the next shop.

If the dealers aren't interested in buying, or tell you, 'These aren't selling at the moment,' simply move on again or ask if they can point you in the direction of someone who might be able help you.

Auctions

Most auction houses now advertise their catalogues in advance on the Internet, so they can attract buyers from around the world. This is to the advantage of the seller because there are many more potential buyers, and there is no limit to what they might pay.

It is common for most big auction houses to have a floor limit, which means that if your item isn't of high enough value, it won't be accepted for sale. You might, however, be referred to another auction house that has a lower floor limit.

How do auctions work?

Quite simply, you take your item to the auction house, or a representative comes to you if the item is large, and you are given a free estimate of its value.

Let's say you have a chest of drawers estimated at £250–£290. If you agree, you can decide on your own reserve price or take the advice of the auction house. If you genuinely want to sell the item, don't be greedy when setting a reserve. Ask the house to set a 'will sell' reserve to ensure a sale.

Now let's say that your chest sells for £280. From that you must deduct the auction house commission of around 15 per cent, plus 1 per cent for insurance and 17.5 per cent VAT (applicable to the insurance only). This means that the cheque you receive about one week after the auction will be for £194.

If you were to sell the same chest to an antique dealer, you might get £200 for it, and receive cash on collection. If the dealer already has a potential buyer who is prepared to pay the full retail value, you might get £280 or more.

Reserve prices

If you are considering selling through an auction house, ask if the company uses auctioneer's discretion, which involves selling an item below the reserve price if the final bid seems fair. You might not want to do this if the reserve price is your absolute minimum.

If your item fails to sell – and this can happen if the sale is poorly attended – it might be automatically re-entered for the next sale with no reserve price. Check the small print in your agreement to see if this is the case. Note too that there may be storage charges for unsold items.

Newspaper advertisements

Let me tell you about the people who advertise in the Wanted ads. First, there are runners – that is, dealers who don't hold stock but run from shop to shop selling items and making perhaps only £10 profit on each sale. They sometimes advertise for stock in newspapers and will often take an item on a sale or return basis. Occasionally, if they can't strike a profitable deal with a shop, they will sell an item without making a penny in order to engender good will.

If the newspaper ads give only a mobile telephone number, my advice is to steer well clear as there are many fly-by-nights around. If you get a dealer to visit you, make sure he has a business card that includes a landline phone number.

Of course, there's nothing to stop sellers from placing their own advertisements in the papers, but I'm not a great fan of this. First, if the item sells quickly, you can still be getting calls about it weeks later. Second, some dishonest people answer newspaper ads as a way of looking at your valuables and checking the security on your property.

If you do decide to sell this way, take the following precautions:

- Get a contact phone number for the person coming to see you.
- Make an excuse to ring the number to check that it's valid.
- Try to have someone with you during the appointment.
- Put the item for sale in your hallway or garage to avoid the buyer looking around your house.
- Accept cash only and don't allow the item to be taken away without payment in full.
- Never accept a cheque.
- Give the buyer a receipt on which you have written 'Sold as seen'. Keep a copy with their signature on it.

Recycling

As I clear houses and sell antiques, I consider myself something of an authority on recycling. My aim is to find good homes for old objects, so here I pass on my best tips about how to do so.

Most of the ideas are not designed to make you money: by this stage you've probably sold your best items using one of the methods described earlier. The aim here is to do some good with your cast-offs and not add to the problem of landfill.

Charities

Apart from the well-known high street charity shops, there are many other organizations who would be delighted to take your unwanted junk. For ideas, look at Waste Not, a book produced by the Charities Aid Foundation and available in most reference libraries.

Most charities take clothes, shoes, toys, books and household china and glass. Some will even take furniture, but none is keen on electrical goods because they must be tested to comply with safety standards.

Salvage companies

Developing countries are eager recipients of old electrical appliances, including typewriters, sewing machines, computers, TVs, videos, irons, fridges and vacuum cleaners. These are shipped overseas by salvage companies, then repaired and sold locally.

If you have a large quantity of old or broken electrical goods to dispose of, look up salvage companies in Yellow Pages and find out which ones are prepared to collect from you.

Auctions

Christies and Phillips are unlikely to be interested in your household junk, but local auction companies could well be. Most provide free advice and valuation, and will dispose of single items or job lots. Although you might make a little money, you won't get rich – but that's not the point, is it?

Jumble sales

The fine old English institution of jumble sales has been the saving of many a cluttered home. Contact your local Brownie and Cub packs, churches or schools to find out when they're holding their next sale. Some will even collect items from you.

Local authorities

Every local council runs some kind of recycling scheme, providing recycling banks in accessible places such as roadside sites, car parks and supermarkets. Many also offer free collection of household recyclable material such as glass, aluminium and plastic, and of dangerous or bulky items, such as fridges and cookers. Some even have recycling schemes for furniture, which they distribute to those in need.

To find out about the recycling facilities in your area, telephone your local authority for details. You should also find leaflets about the various schemes in your town hall.

Other methods of disposal

Advertise your unwanted belongings in the local paper with the words 'free to collector' and you'll be amazed at the response. In most cases, placing the ad is free.

Offer toys, books and magazines to local hospitals or doctors' and dentists' surgeries.

Give unwanted stationery and computer printouts to local playgroups for the children to draw on. They'll also be glad to receive toys and dressing-up clothes.

The RSPCA and other animal care centres will appreciate your unwanted rabbit hutches, bird cages and petfood bowls.

The local history department in most libraries will be grateful for any old photographs or maps that will add to their information about how the area has changed over the years.

Old spectacles can be given to opticians who send them on to developing countries.

Look out for shoe banks and clothes banks outside local shops.

When all else fails, take your junk to the local tip. This offers safe disposal of old engine oil and car batteries, and recycles everything from garden waste to scrap metal and cardboard.

Remember, it has never been easier to recycle. It's a system that's good for the environment and makes you feel good too.

General recycling information

At the front of your telephone directory, you should find a complete listing of all the recycling facilities in your area, as well as general environmental and conservation information. You can telephone Wasteline on 0870 243 0136 for further information on household recycling.

6

An ounce of prevention

It is a widely held belief in most addiction treatment programmes, that you must hit rock bottom before you can begin the recovery process. Many of the underlying reasons that clutter gets out of control are formed by letting addictive behaviours become part of your daily life. Accepting that there is a problem and taking action to correct it is one of the first steps towards moving on your path to health and happiness.

Those who have given up smoking know how difficult it can be to kick the habit. They also know that as soon as they start smoking again, it returns to its previous level. Addiction means all or nothing.

The same is true for clutter addicts. There is no going back. If you no longer connect to the present moment and see what is going on around you, in all likelihood your house will return to its chaotic state within 12 months. Acknowledge that you are a recovering clutter junkie and develop the self-worth to know that you deserve to to enjoy your surroundings and your life.

One day at a time

I was surprised to learn that the five basic principles of Reiki are very similar to the 12-step programme used by Alcoholics Anonymous. They both begin with the most important words – just for today. By taking one day at a time, you will begin to appreciate the subtle signs around you and be able to see things more clearly.

A clear and focused mind is the surest way to accomplish your goals. In every situation, it is important to focus your attention on what you intend to achieve rather than what you want to achieve. Having the intention allows you to get the job done. Try it and see for yourself.

As you recall each of your clutter issues, remember the lessons learned from each situation. The methods suggested in this book have been tried and tested, and really do work. Once you have truly understood the meaning of each situation, you will be able to let go of your mental and emotional attachments to it. Once released, they do not return.

Taking stock

Having shed all your clutter, it is now time to take stock of the things you own. You have chosen them to be part of your life, so stay focused and use them or lose them.

Many of the exercises you have been through to let things go suggest that you review the situation after a period of time. Start with the recommended time in each exercise – usually four weeks. If the situation has remained clutter-free, make your next review in eight weeks' time. Keep doubling the amount of time between reviews as long as you have not reverted to bad habits. If you find that you have slipped back into old routines, revisit the situation in half the amount of recommended time, repeating the procedure until things are under control again.

Surveying progress

In order to move forward, it is important to understand where you came from. The Life Laundry Survey in Chapter 1 was designed to give you a starting point to look at clutter issues objectively and to gain an understanding of how they affected your life at the time of the survey.

When you feel that you have tackled and controlled those areas in your life that were overtaken by clutter, go back to the survey and have another look. Viewed from today's perspective, how have your patterns and behaviours changed? Sit down and do the survey again, this time imagining your life in the present moment. See if you are able to lower your scores.

Review the goals that you set in the short, medium and long term. See how many of them you achieved. Look at what you managed by way of fulfilling the remainder. Did you remember to think about your intention? Go back to the problem-solving section on pages 38–41 and think about what got in the way.

Assessing the benefits

Has your health improved as a result of getting rid of all the physical and emotional energy blockages in your house? Go back to the energy assessment part of the survey on pages 31–2 and see if your energy levels are different since reducing the clutter. In most cases there will be a dramatic improvement.

Are you now able to use each room for its intended purpose? Does it make you feel more grounded knowing where things are and where they need to be? Have you been able to reclaim extra space for living? How has it changed your view of your home?

Look again at the list of hobbies you still had a desire to pursue. Have you managed to fit them into your daily routine? If not, bring your awareness to the situation and know that you can achieve whatever you wish. Undertake the process today and do it. One step at a time.

Suggested reading

A Path with Heart, Jack Kornfield, Bantam Books, 1993.

Awaken the Giant Within, Anthony Robbins, Pocket Books, 1992.

Calm at Work, Paul Wilson, Penguin Books, 1998.

Clear Your Clutter with Feng Shui, Karen Kingston, Piatkus, 1998.

Don't Sweat the Small Stuff, Richard Carlson, Hodder & Stoughton, 1998.

Essential Reiki, Diane Stein, Crossing Press, 1995.

Hands of Light, Barbara Ann Brennan, Bantam USA, 1990.

Initimate Death, Marie De Hennezel, Little, Brown & Company, 1997.

Mary Ellen's Complete Home Reference Book,
    Mary Ellen Pinkham with Dale Burgh, Three Rivers Press, 1994.

Natural Superwoman, Rosamond Richardson, Kyle Cathie, 1999.

New Leaf New Life, Dawna Walter, Quadrille Publishing Ltd, 2001.

Organized Living, Dawna Walter and Helen Chislett, Conran Octopus, 1997.

Reiki – Practical Ways to Harmony, Mari Hall, HarperCollins, 2000.

The Feng Shui House Book,
    Gina Lazenby and William Speer, Conran Octopus, 1998.

The Meaning of Things – Applying Philosophy to Life,
    A.C. Grayling, Weidenfeld, 2001.

The Mind-Body Workout, Lynne Robinson and Helge Fisher, Pan, 1998.

The Seven Spiritual Laws of Success,
    Deepak Chopra, Amber-Allen Publishing, 1995.

The Seven Habits of Highly Effective People, Stephen R. Covey,
    Simon & Schuster, 1999.

The Ultimate Book of Household Hints & Tips,
    Cassandra Kent, Dorling Kindersley, 1996.

Vibrational Medicine,
    Richard Gerber, M.D., Bear & Company, 2001 (3rd ed.).

Useful organizations

Helplines

Bereavement
- Cruse Bereavement Line
  National line: 0870 167 1677
  http://www.caritas.data.co.uk

Emotional Support
- Samaritans
  0845 790 9090
  http://www.samaritans.org.uk

Check your local phone directory under Charitable & Voluntary Organisations and Charity Shops.

Alternative Therapies

Aromatherapy
- International Federation of Aromatherapists
  Call for information on how to obtain local practitioners.
  020 8742 2605
  http://www.int-fed-aromatherapy.co.uk

Crystal Healing
- Affiliation of Crystal Healing Organisations
  P.O. Box 100, Exminster, Exeter
  01479 841450

Flower Remedies
- Dr Edward Bach Centre
  Mount Vernon, Sotwell, Wallingford
  Oxfordshire OX10 1PZ
  01491 834678
  http://www.backcentre.com

Homeopathy
- Society of Homeopaths
  4a Artizan Road, Northampton NN1
  01604 621400
  http://www.homeopathy-soh.org

Light Therapy
- SAD Association (SADA)
  PO Box 989, Steyning BN44 3HG
  01903 814942
  http://www.sada-org.uk

Meditation
- Transcendental Meditation
  Call for details of your nearest centre
  0800 269 303
  http://www.t-m.org.uk

Reiki
- Dr Allan J. Sweeney International Reiki Healing and Training Centre
  10 Beach Houses, Royal Crescent
  Margate, Kent CT9 5AL
  01843 230377
  http://www.reiki-healing.com

Stress Management
- International Stress Management Association
  P.O. Box 348, Waltham Crescent EN8 8ZL
  07000 780430
  http://www.isma.org.uk

Yoga
- The British Wheel of Yoga
  25 Jermyn Street, Sleaford
  Lincolnshire NG34 7RU
  01529 306851
  http://www.bwy.org.uk

Index

Acknowledgements

Dedicated to Leah Franks and Celia Jane Dowell.

This book would not be possible without the tremendously talented and creative team involved with the production of the book and television series.

Mark and I both would like to thank everyone at BBC Books – Robin Wood, Nicky Copeland, Sarah Lavelle, Lisa Pettibone and Victoria Hall for being such great enthusiasts of the project. We would also like to thank Cat Ledger from Talkback for helping to get the project off the ground.

The Talkback Production team seems like family to both of us. Working on such an intense project brings out the strength in each and every member of the team. Our unreserved thanks for putting up with two novices.

Daisy Goodwin, Susie Worster, Ian Liddington, Esther Lochrie, Caroline Frazer, Amelia Dare, Tony Tackaberry, Claire Sweeney, Perry Harrison, Tim Cragg, Chris Kenny, Justin Evans, Nikki Williams, Johanna Fry, Matt, Vics Elson, Sally Gray, Bella Whitely, James De Frond, Matt Gray, Geoff Glencross, Pat Waters, Neil Callow, Sam Brock, Jamie Brooks, Tex and Rob and all of our soundmen for the series.

We would also like to thank the following for their contributions to the programme: Black & Decker, DeWalt, Elephant, Flokati Rug Company, Homebase, Honda, Nava Office Accessories, Paperchase, Screwfix Direct, The Pier and Tombu UK Ltd.

Most importantly, our heartfelt thanks to all of our contributors who let us into their lives to make the series: Delores, Paul, Katy, Carolyn, James, Kathryn, Ann, Ollie, Liz, Derek, Olivia, Adam, Philippa, Bryonnie, Neil, Kaye, John and Gillie.

I would like to say a special word of thanks to my Reiki Master, Allan Sweeney for teaching me many of the methods that I have shared in this book. I must also thank my husband for his great editing skills, Kate Stobbs for editing my life during this process and Christopher Felstead for past omissions.

Mark would like to thank his family and his wife, Lisa.